SOLID TRUTH
for Slippery Times

An Inductive Journey Through Galatians

by

pam gillaspie

Galatians: Solid Truth for Slippery Times

Copyright © 2013 by Pam Gillaspie
Published by Precept Ministries
International
P.O. Box 182218
Chattanooga, Tennessee 37422
www.precept.org

ISBN 978-1-62119-147-6

Printed in the United States of America

2013

Dedicated to . . .

Mom and Dad Gillaspie. Thank you for your constant love and unceasing prayers. They mean the world to me!

Acknowledgements

Although this is the first paragraph of the book, it is always the last paragraph that I write as I look back and consider the way God works in using so many different people to bring a study together. I'm just one of the tools in His hand. This study—and all of my studies so far—began with a patient group of women piloting a class with me at my local church. Thanks to each of my classmates for walking the road and enduring the vertical white board and the unedited product with me.

Rick and Pete, thank you for your consistent editing, teaching, and coaching as we've worked through so many manuscripts together over the years. I learn and am sharpened with every project and I am grateful. Cress, thanks for your availability and speed in proofreading. Dave, as always, thank you for the cover design and for putting up with me in the press-readying process. Finally, thanks so much to Staci, BJ, David, Brian, John, Scott, and Paula for all of your work in design, marketing, and getting the message out. You have no idea how grateful I am to be part of such a talented team!

Galatians
Solid Truth for Slippery Times

Galatians: SOLID TRUTH for Slippery Times

Contents

There is nothing quite like your favorite pair of jeans. You can dress them up, you can dress them down. You can work in them, play in them, shop in them . . . live in them. They always feel right. It is my hope that the structure of this Bible study will fit you like those jeans; that it will work with your life right now, right where you are whether you're new to this whole Bible thing or whether you've been studying the Book for years!

How is this even be possible? Smoke and mirrors, perhaps? The new mercilessly thrown in the deep end? The experienced given pompoms and the job of simply cheering others on? None of the above.

Sweeter than Chocolate!® flexible studies are designed with options that will allow you to go as deep each week as you desire. If you're just starting out and feeling a little overwhelmed, stick with the main text and don't think a second thought about the sidebar assignments. If you're looking for a challenge, then take the sidebar prompts and go ahead and dig all the way to China! As you move along through the study, think of the sidebars and "Digging Deeper" boxes as that 2% of lycra that you find in certain jeans . . . the wiggle-room that will help them fit just right.

Beginners may find that they want to start adding in some of the optional assignments as they go along. Experts may find that when three children are throwing up for three days straight, foregoing those assignments for the week is the way to live wisely.

Life has a way of ebbing and flowing and this study is designed to ebb and flow right along with it!

Enjoy!

Sweeter than Chocolate!® studies meet you where you are and take you as far as you want to go.

WEEKLY STUDY: The main text guides you through the complete topic of study for the week.

FYI boxes: For Your Information boxes provide bite-sized material to shed additional light on the topic.

FYI:

Reading Tip: Begin with prayer
You may have heard this a million times over and if this is a million and one, so be it. Whenever you read or study God's Word, first pray and ask His Spirit to be your Guide.

ONE STEP FURTHER and other sidebar boxes: Sidebar boxes give you the option to push yourself a little further. If you have extra time or are looking for an extra challenge, you can try one, all, or any number in between! These boxes give you the ultimate in flexibility.

ONE STEP FURTHER:

Word Study: *torah*/law
The first of eight Hebrew key words we encounter for God's Word is *torah* translated "law." If you're up for a challenge this week, do a word study to learn what you can about *torah*. Run a concordance search and examine where the word *torah* appears in the Old Testament and see what you can learn from the contexts.

If you decide to look for the word for "law" in the New Testament, you'll find that the primary Greek word is *nomos*.

Be sure to see what Paul says about the law in Galatians 3 and what Jesus says in Matthew 5.

DIGGING DEEPER boxes: If you're looking to go further, Digging Deeper sections will help you sharpen your skills as you continue to mine the truths of Scripture for yourself.

Digging Deeper

What else does God's Word say about counselors?

If you can, spend some time this week digging around for what God's Word says about counselors.

Start by considering what you already know about counsel from the Word of God and see if you can actually show where these truths are in the Bible. Make sure that the Word actually says what you think it says.

A Misplaced Zeal and a Twisted Gospel

As we have said before, so I say again now, if any man is preaching to you a gospel contrary to what you received, he is to be accursed!
–Galatians 1:9

Relativism. Tolerance. Living your own truth. We live in slippery times, in times where truth has stumbled, where everyone does what is right in his or her own eyes. Absolutes have been shown the door not only in the public square but often in the Church as well. Experience rules the day in many hearts and minds and the pure truth of the Gospel has all too often been shelved in favor of man's programs and procedures, rules and ways. Man in his zeal likes to control. But man's ways are not God's ways.

The letter to the Galatians overflows with examples of man's ways colliding with God's ways. This week, we'll overview the entire letter and then focus our attention on Galatians 1 as we see the apostle Paul ground his authority in his call, not from fallen man but from Almighty God.

FYI:

If You're in a Class
Complete **Week One** together on your first day of class. This will be a great way to start getting to know one another and will help those who are newer to Bible study get their bearings.

CONSIDER the WAY you THINK

As we begin our study together, we're going to look at the whole letter of Galatians reading it through several times before we go back and examine it more thoroughly chapter by chapter. We'll start by simply reading through Galatians at least three times this week. If possible use an NAS or ESV Bible for one of your readings. Also (trust me here), select a paraphrase to read. All versions should be easily accessible online if you don't have extra Bibles around the house. Try to do each read-through in a single sitting.

WEEKLY READ-THROUGH #1

Version I read:

Main observations:

Big questions:

NASB and ESV

The NASB and ESV are two of the most reliable word-for-word translations from the original languages. While the KJV and NKJV are also translated word for word, they do not include consideration of earlier-dated original-language manuscripts discovered more recently.

WEEKLY READ-THROUGH #2

Version I read:

Main observations:

Big questions:

WEEKLY READ-THROUGH #3

Version I read:

Main observations:

Big questions:

FYI:

Start with Prayer

You've probably heard it before and if we study together in the future, you're sure to hear it again. Whenever you read or study God's Word, first pray and ask His Spirit to be your Guide. Jesus says that the Spirit will lead us into all truth.

Galatians
Solid Truth for Slippery Times

DISCUSS with your GROUP or PONDER on your own . . .

As you read, were you aware of any presuppositions you brought to the text? Do you have views that predisposed you toward a particular interpretation? If so, jot them down.

What differences did you notice between the translations?

What differences did you notice between the translations and the paraphrase?

Was the paraphrase easier to understand? Did it differ substantially from the word-for-word translations?

WHO, WHAT, WHEN, WHERE, WHY, and HOW

Who wrote Galatians? Who was he writing to? (author and recipients)

What kind of writing is this? (genre)

A Region, Not a City

Galatians is written not to one church in a single city but to the churches in the region of Galatia. Because Paul wrote other epistles to cities it's easy to assume there is a city of Galatia. To my simple mind it's kind of like baseball, most teams—like the Chicago Cubs and the Seattle Mariners—are associated with a single city, but others like the Minnesota Twins are associated with a region, in this case a state.

When was Galatians written? What timing clues are we given in the text? (This one is disputed.)

Where was the author writing from? Can we know for certain? Why/why not? (origin)

Where were the recipients located? (destination)

Why did Paul write Galatians? (occasion)

How does the Galatian account (2:1-10) of the Jerusalem Council square with Luke's account in Acts 15? What questions do the two accounts raise?

FYI:

Northern/Southern Galatian Theories

Answering the question *Who are the recipients of this letter?* is often a slam-dunk. Paul wrote the Corinthian letters to the church in the city of Corinth, Philippians to the church in the city of Philippi, Colossians to the church at the city of Colossae. He addresses Galatians, however, to the churches of Galatia. The letter is often referred to as a circular letter, meaning that it was intended to be read by one church and then passed along to the next one.

The Galatian theories hinge on how Paul used the term "Galatians." Was he referring to people in the northern section of the land or to the Roman province in the south?

If he is writing to churches in the Roman province of Galatia they include those that Paul and Barnabas planted on their first missionary journey—Derbe, Lystra, Iconium, and Pisidian Antioch (Acts 18:23).

While commentaries often address this as a "major" question, the answer does not affect the theology of the Galatian letter.

If you have the time and the interest, check out a good commentary to see what the scholars say about who the Galatians were and when the letter was written. While the answers don't affect the message of Galatians, the information may help you relate the writing to what you read in Acts.

Galatians
Solid Truth for Slippery Times

Digging Deeper

Comparing Translations and Paraphrases

This is not for the faint of heart. Pick one verse from Galatians where you find a significant difference between two translations or between a translation and a paraphrased verse and compare it against the Greek text to see where the variations come from. For those who wonder why the translations differ so much, take the time to work through this assignment. If you have access to Logos or are comfortable in the original languages, have at it. If not, here is some direction to help you on your way.

Website: www.interlinearbible.org

Select: Greek/English Interlinear

Operating Instructions:

At the top of the page, type in Galatians 1 (or whatever verse you're looking for). The page will return the Greek text of your search verse along with the Greek part of speech and English translation. For each word, you'll see something like this:

Strong Number and Englishman's occurrences . . . . .4957 [e]
Transliterated Greek word .synestauromai
Actual Greek text . . . . συνεσταυρωμαι
Translated text . . . . .I have been crucified with
Verb Parsing Information .V-RIM/P-1S
(In this case: Verb–Perfect, Indicative, Middle or Passive–1st person singular)

Website: www.biblestudytools.com

Select: Parallel Bible

Operating Instructions:

In the search window entitled "Search Online Parallel Bible," type the verse you're comparing. You can opt to compare specific versions side by side or compare all the versions available on the site.

FYI:

Early or Late Date?

The recipients Paul addressed (northern or southern Galatia) impacts the letter's dating. Those who believe the letter is addressed to ethnic Galatians further north place a late date on Galatians based on Luke's account in the book of Acts.

If Paul's audience was the churches of Derbe, Lystra, Iconium and Pisidian Antioch, however, a much earlier date is possible. Many scholars think Galatians is Paul's earliest existing letter and date it cAD48 or 49.

While the dating of Galatians is a hot topic among scholars, it doesn't impact the message of the letter. As a student it's important to know that while we can't answer every inductive question we raise, God's Word is clear even when we can't fill in all the blanks.

Galatians
Solid Truth for Slippery Times

Questions to Consider:

Where do the translations/paraphrases stick closely to the original language?

Where do they diverge?

Do the different translations and paraphrases contradict each other's propositions (e.g., "God is holy" versus "God is not holy") or do they offer shades of meaning to each other's terms (e.g., "In the beginning was the Word" versus "In the beginning the Word already existed")?

What else have you observed?

FYI:

The Churches in Galatia
We can often remember more easily when we tie new information into a familiar format—old information in modern packaging if you will. For recall, let's think of our Galatian cities in a "city, state" format:

Pisidian Antioch, Galatia

Iconium, Galatia

Lystra, Galatia

Derbe, Galatia

Others you might want to remember . . .

Philippi, Macedonia

Thessalonica, Macedonia

Berea, Macedonia

Ephesus, Asia

Colossae, Asia

Pergamum, Asia

Smyrna, Asia

Galatians
Solid Truth for Slippery Times

GALATIANS 1

In Galatians 1 Paul establishes his apostleship, coolly greets the Galatians, and quickly jumps to the bottom line of his purpose for writing.

OBSERVE the TEXT of SCRIPTURE

READ Galatians 1 and **MARK** key, repeated words in a distinctive fashion.

Galatians 1

1   Paul, an apostle (not sent *from men nor through the agency of man, but through Jesus Christ and God the Father, who raised Him from the dead*),

2   and all the brethren who are with me,

    To the churches of Galatia:

3   Grace to you and peace from God our Father and the Lord Jesus Christ,

4   who gave Himself for our sins so that He might rescue us from this present evil age, according to the will of our God and Father,

5   to whom be the glory forevermore. Amen.

6   I am amazed that you are so quickly deserting Him who called you by the grace of Christ, for a different gospel;

7   which is really not another; only there are some who are disturbing you and want to distort the gospel of Christ.

8   But even if we, or an angel from heaven, should preach to you a gospel contrary to what we have preached to you, he is to be accursed!

9   As we have said before, so I say again now, if any man is preaching to you a gospel contrary to what you received, he is to be accursed!

10 For am I now seeking the favor of men, or of God? Or am I striving to please men? If I were still trying to please men, I would not be a bond-servant of Christ.

11 For I would have you know, brethren, that the gospel which was preached by me is not according to man.

12 For I neither received it from man, nor was I taught it, but I received it through a revelation of Jesus Christ.

13 For you have heard of my former manner of life in Judaism, how I used to persecute the church of God beyond measure and tried to destroy it;

14 and I was advancing in Judaism beyond many of my contemporaries among my countrymen, being more extremely zealous for my ancestral traditions.

15 But when God, who had set me apart even from my mother's womb and called me through His grace, was pleased

16 to reveal His Son in me so that I might preach Him among the Gentiles, I did not immediately consult with flesh and blood,

17 nor did I go up to Jerusalem to those who were apostles before me; but I went away to Arabia, and returned once more to Damascus.

Charis and Shalom

"Grace (*charis*) and peace (*eirene / shalom*)" merge together a typical Greek greeting with a common Jewish one.

Marking the Text

You'll find some key words to mark on the next page, but it's better for everyone— and loads more fun for you!—if you can begin identifying them for yourself.

Galatians
Solid Truth for Slippery Times

18 *Then three years later I went up to Jerusalem to become acquainted with Cephas, and stayed with him fifteen days.*

19 *But I did not see any other of the apostles except James, the Lord's brother.*

20 *(Now in what I am writing to you, I assure you before God that I am not lying.)*

21 *Then I went into the regions of Syria and Cilicia.*

22 *I was still unknown by sight to the churches of Judea which were in Christ;*

23 *but only, they kept hearing, "He who once persecuted us is now preaching the faith which he once tried to destroy."*

24 *And they were glorifying God because of me.*

DISCUSS with your GROUP or PONDER on your own . . .

What did you initially observe from the text?

What key words did you notice?

What did you learn about Paul? How does he describe his changed life?

ONE STEP FURTHER:

Check Out Paul's History in Acts

If you have some extra time this week, learn more about Paul by reading or listening to Luke's account in the Acts of the Apostles. The unconverted Paul, then known as Saul, first enters the biblical scene in Acts 7:58 when those martyring Stephen lay their coats at his feet. Subsequent chapters recount his persecution of believers, his conversion, and eventually his life of ministry. Record below your Saul/Paul observations from the book of Acts.

FYI:

Don't Be Afraid to Ask Questions

He can answer. You won't undo Him.

Galatians
Solid Truth for Slippery Times

LOOKING CLOSER . . .
OBSERVE the TEXT of SCRIPTURE

READ Galatians 1:1-5 and **MARK** references to *Paul*, *God*, and *men*.

Galatians 1

1 *Paul, an apostle (not* sent *from men nor through the agency of man, but through Jesus Christ and God the Father, who raised Him from the dead),*

2 *and all the brethren who are with me,*

   To the churches of Galatia:

3 *Grace to you and peace from God our Father and the Lord Jesus Christ,*

4 *who gave Himself for our sins so that He might rescue us from this present evil age, according to the will of our God and Father,*

5 *to whom be the glory forevermore. Amen.*

DISCUSS with your GROUP or PONDER on your own . . .

How did Paul become an apostle? What had nothing to do with his apostleship?

What theological points does Paul drive home in these opening verses particularly with regard to Jesus? To God the Father?

Why did Jesus give Himself over for our sins?

What does this tell us about the seriousness of our situation apart from Him?

FYI:

It's Not Going to Get Better

If you run into teaching that suggests things are going to get dramatically better on earth before Jesus returns, go back and compare the teaching with Scripture.

Do you typically hear the Gospel presented against the backdrop of coming judgment? Explain.

ONE STEP FURTHER:

What will the last days look like?

The author of Hebrews tells us that "in these last days" God has spoken to us in His Son. Writing in the first century AD, he includes his generation in last days. As we move toward the end of the last days, the Word tells us what we can expect both from human nature in general and, more specifically, from the generations between the appearings of Christ. It is not butterflies and rainbows. This week, if you have some extra time, examine what God's Word says we can expect to see before the return of Jesus. Here are a few passages to get you started, but don't feel limited to these:

2 Timothy 3

2 Peter 3

1 John 2

Jude

Revelation 1–3

How specifically does Paul describe the "age" he's in? How does this compare with our age?

How big a deal is the true Gospel based on God's investment in it?

Galatians
Solid Truth for Slippery Times

Digging Deeper

The Other Greetings

Paul's displeasure with the Galatian churches is apparent in what he says in his letter. If you have some time this week, compare Paul's curt address "to the churches of Galatia" with his greetings in other letters.

Romans

1 Corinthians

2 Corinthians

Ephesians

Philippians

Colossians

1 Thessalonians

2 Thessalonians

1 Timothy

2 Timothy

Titus

Philemon

OBSERVE the TEXT of SCRIPTURE

READ Galatians 1:6-10 and **MARK** references to *Paul, God, men,* and *gospel/ another gospel.*

6 *I am amazed that you are so quickly deserting Him who called you by the grace of Christ, for a different gospel;*

7 *which is really not another; only there are some who are disturbing you and want to distort the gospel of Christ.*

8 *But even if we, or an angel from heaven, should preach to you a gospel contrary to what we have preached to you, he is to be accursed!*

9 *As we have said before, so I say again now, if any man is preaching to you a gospel contrary to what you received, he is to be accursed!*

10 *For am I now seeking the favor of men, or of God? Or am I striving to please men? If I were still trying to please men, I would not be a bond-servant of Christ.*

DISCUSS with your GROUP or PONDER on your own . . .

What has Paul already established about the true Gospel according to Galatians 1:1-5?

How does Paul open this section? What amazes him?

In distorting the true Gospel, what are these people actually doing? Is it more than just confusing the facts? Explain.

ONE STEP FURTHER:

Word Study: Persecution

If you have time this week, see if you can find the Greek word group for *persecute/persecution.* How does it relate to Paul in Galatians 1 and how does it relate to what Christians can expect if they live godly in Christ Jesus? Record your findings below.

FYI:

Too open-ended?

My goal with open-ended questions—particularly in **Digging Deeper** sections—is to challenge you to think for yourself without depending on prompts. Over time this will help you reason through the text more and more for yourself. I believe you'll discover more if you're given more room to ask questions and explore. If you only have to fill in a blank, that's about how much you'll learn . . . but if you're given a page, oh my, the possibilities are endless!

Galatians
Solid Truth for Slippery Times

How does Paul consistently refer to the false teaching? What does he contrast it with? What does this suggest about what they had already received?

How open are people today to "a gospel contrary" to the one the Apostles preached? Do our churches recognize a "gospel contrary"? Do you? How?

What repeated phrase does Paul use to say what should happen to those who distort the Gospel?

What is precluded in being a bond-servant of Christ? Applications?

How does the tension between pleasing men and God reveal itself in your life? In your church?

Mid-Week Review . . .

Summarize the basics of Paul's words so far in Galatians 1:1-10.

What is his main point in Galatians 1:1-10?

INDUCTIVE FOCUS:

Questioning the Text

The key to exegesis (the fancy word meaning to draw meaning out of Scripture) is questioning the text. The basic investigative questions *Who? What? When? Where? Why?* and *How?* are your framework. Not every question can be addressed to every verse, and most verses require several variations on the same question. As we study God's Word together, realize that not every question that can be asked will be asked, but don't let that stop you from asking other questions and exploring further on your own. We will never run out of questions to ask and answers to glean from God's Word!

If you're at a loss for what questions to ask, pay attention to the words that you've marked. Go to your key words and start there with your questions! Marking helps you see the main idea and frame questions.

OBSERVE the TEXT of SCRIPTURE

Paul writes a lengthy autobiographical section in his letter that runs from Galatians 1:11 to the middle of Galatians 2. His status as a true apostle of Jesus Christ is critical to his argument that the Gospel he proclaims is authoritative.

READ Galatians 1:11-14. Continue to **MARK** *gospel*, *man*, and their synonyms. Also mark every negative reference you see (*not, neither, nor*).

11 *For I would have you know, brethren, that the gospel which was preached by me is not according to man.*

12 *For I neither received it from man, nor was I taught it, but I received it through a revelation of Jesus Christ.*

13 *For you have heard of my former manner of life in Judaism, how I used to persecute the church of God beyond measure and tried to destroy it;*

14 *and I was advancing in Judaism beyond many of my contemporaries among my countrymen, being more extremely zealous for my ancestral traditions.*

Galatians
Solid Truth for Slippery Times

DISCUSS with your GROUP or PONDER on your own . . .

What additional information do these verses tell us about the Gospel Paul preaches? Where did this gospel come from? Where did it *not* come from?

First Century Judaism

In Galatians 1 Paul talks about his rapid advancement in Judaism. You'll learn quite a bit about first century Judaism simply by reading Galatians. If you have time this week, though, and want to do some additional research, see what you can find out about what Paul's life as a first century Jew was. Biblical cross-references and Bible dictionaries are a couple of good places to start. Record your findings below.

How does this compare with the source of Paul's apostleship? What implications can we draw from this?

Based on the witness of the rest of Scripture, did Paul's Gospel "match" what the original apostles taught? Explain.

The Triple Negative

Paul's use of the triple negative cocktail—*not, neither, nor*—in verses 11 and 12 adds emphasis to the statement that his Gospel was not human in origin.

Are Paul's words authoritative? Why? How do they compare with those of the people who are bringing a different gospel?

Galatians
Solid Truth for Slippery Times

What does Paul reveal about his "former manner of life in Judaism"? How did he treat the church?

What characterized his behavior? What words or phrases does he use to describe that time in his life?

Have you ever exhibited misplaced zeal? (Not sure how to ask this one gently!) How and what did you sow? What did you reap?

How do you know if your zeal is on track? How can you measure or evaluate it?

ONE STEP FURTHER:

Word Study: Revelation
If you have some extra time this week, find the Greek word translated *revelation* in Galatians 1:12. Where else does the word group appear in Galatians 1? How does Paul use this word? How is it used elsewhere in the New Testament? Record your findings below.

FYI

Priests Who Turned to the Faith
The word of God kept on spreading; and the number of the disciples continued to increase greatly in Jerusalem, and a great many of the priests were becoming obedient to the faith.

—Acts 6:7

Galatians
Solid Truth for Slippery Times

Digging Deeper

What is the Gospel?

Paul goes to the mat in Galatians over the Gospel of Jesus Christ. What is the Gospel message? How is the Gospel defined in God's Word? This week, if you're up for a challenge, scour the pages of Scripture to see how the Gospel is defined, described, and explained.

What glimpses of the Gospel do we see in the Old Testament?

How is the Gospel message proclaimed in the synoptic Gospels Matthew, Mark, and Luke?

How does this compare with the proclamation in John's Gospel?

INDUCTIVE FOCUS:

What is a Key Word?

A key word or key phrase unlocks the meaning of a text. Key words are sometimes repeated and are critical to the message of the passage.

In Galatians 1 *gospel* is clearly a key word but there are others. Did you notice any of them? If so, record them below as well as what you learned.

If not, read back through the text watching for words that cluster within a few verses and are key to making sense of the text. If you don't see them right away, don't worry. I'll help by pointing out some as we go.

Identifying key words is a skill that develops over time, but you practice by observing carefully—so keep your eyes open. You will get it! Keep praying and keep looking.

What do we learn about the Gospel in Paul's writing?

What do other New Testament writers say about the Gospel?

What is the Gospel?

How would you explain the Gospel to a friend?

Galatians
Solid Truth for Slippery Times

CONTEXT

In the next section of Galatians 1, verses 15-24, Paul talks about God revealing His Son in him. To put us in context, let's look at the account of Paul's conversion on the road to Damascus. Note that the text refers to him by his Hebrew name, Saul.

OBSERVE the TEXT of SCRIPTURE

READ Acts 9:1-16 and **MARK** every reference to *Saul* (i.e., Paul) including pronouns.

1 Now Saul, still breathing threats and murder against the disciples of the Lord, went to the high priest,

2 and asked for letters from him to the synagogues at Damascus, so that if he found any belonging to the Way, both men and women, he might bring them bound to Jerusalem.

3 As he was traveling, it happened that he was approaching Damascus, and suddenly a light from heaven flashed around him;

4 and he fell to the ground and heard a voice saying to him, "Saul, Saul, why are you persecuting Me?"

5 And he said, "Who are You, Lord?" And He said, "I am Jesus whom you are persecuting,

6 but get up and enter the city, and it will be told you what you must do."

7 The men who traveled with him stood speechless, hearing the voice but seeing no one.

8 Saul got up from the ground, and though his eyes were open, he could see nothing; and leading him by the hand, they brought him into Damascus.

9 And he was three days without sight, and neither ate nor drank.

10 Now there was a disciple at Damascus named Ananias; and the Lord said to him in a vision, "Ananias." And he said, "Here I am, Lord."

11 And the Lord said to him, "Get up and go to the street called Straight, and inquire at the house of Judas for a man from Tarsus named Saul, for he is praying,

12 and he has seen in a vision a man named Ananias come in and lay his hands on him, so that he might regain his sight."

13 But Ananias answered, "Lord, I have heard from many about this man, how much harm he did to Your saints at Jerusalem;

14 and here he has authority from the chief priests to bind all who call on Your name."

15 But the Lord said to him, "Go, for he is a chosen instrument of Mine, to bear My name before the Gentiles and kings and the sons of Israel;

16 for I will show him how much he must suffer for My name's sake."

Galatians
Solid Truth for Slippery Times

DISCUSS with your GROUP or PONDER on your own . . .

What does Luke tell his readers about Saul's pre-conversion behavior?

What does he quote Ananias saying about Saul?

What is Saul up to at the beginning of Acts 9?

Where has he been and where is he going? For what purpose?

What happens to him on the road? What does he see? What does he hear?

How do his companions perceive the event?

ONE STEP FURTHER:

Set Apart from the Womb

If you have some extra time this week, see if you can find other biblical characters who were called and set apart before they were born. Record your findings below.

What does Jesus say to Saul?

Authentication

A key principle we see throughout Acts is authentication. Over and over again when one person hears a supernatural message, another person hears a corresponding message that authenticates the veracity of both.

What happens to Saul physically as a result of his encounter on the road?

What does the Lord tell Ananias in a vision?

Unless the Father Draws

"No one can come to Me unless the Father who sent Me draws him; and I will raise him up on the last day."

—Jesus, John 6:44

How does Ananias respond? What are his concerns?

How does God answer? What are His plans for Saul?

Describe Saul's conversion. Did Saul seek God or did God seek Saul? What do you make of this? Does this make you rethink anything regarding man's approach to God or the church's approach to evangelism? Explain your reasoning.

Digging Deeper

And you will be My witnesses . . .

We've already spent time this week looking at what the Gospel is. This **Digging Deeper** section is a follow-up. What are we to do with the message? The Bible is clear that Jesus' followers are to be witnesses. In fact, Jesus' final words before returning to heaven—recorded in Matthew 28:18-20 and Acts 1:7-8—command His followers to do just that.

Matthew 28:18b-20

"All authority has been given to Me in heaven and on earth. Go therefore and make disciples of all the nations, baptizing them in the name of the Father and the Son and the Holy Spirit, teaching them to observe all that I commanded you; and lo, I am with you always, even to the end of the age."

Acts 1:7b-8

"It is not for you to know times or epochs which the Father has fixed by His own authority; but you will receive power when the Holy Spirit has come upon you; and you shall be My witnesses both in Jerusalem, and in all Judea and Samaria, and even to the remotest part of the earth."

If you have some extra time this week, examine these questions from a biblical perspective using whatever study resources you have at your disposal.

What is a witness?

What does a witness do? Is there anything a witness can't do? Explain.

Galatians
Solid Truth for Slippery Times

OBSERVE the TEXT of SCRIPTURE

READ Galatians 1:15-24 and **MARK** every reference to Paul and to God.

15 *But when God, who had set me apart even from my mother's womb and called me through His grace, was pleased*

16 *to reveal His Son in me so that I might preach Him among the Gentiles, I did not immediately consult with flesh and blood,*

17 *nor did I go up to Jerusalem to those who were apostles before me; but I went away to Arabia, and returned once more to Damascus.*

18 *Then three years later I went up to Jerusalem to become acquainted with Cephas, and stayed with him fifteen days.*

19 *But I did not see any other of the apostles except James, the Lord's brother.*

20 *(Now in what I am writing to you, I assure you before God that I am not lying.)*

21 *Then I went into the regions of Syria and Cilicia.*

22 *I was still unknown by sight to the churches of Judea which were in Christ;*

23 *but only, they kept hearing, "He who once persecuted us is now preaching the faith which he once tried to destroy."*

24 *And they were glorifying God because of me.*

DISCUSS with your GROUP or PONDER on your own . . .

At what point did Paul belong to God? Explain your reasoning.

What does Paul say about God's role in his salvation?

How does this square with your view of how people come into relationship with Christ? Explain.

Cephas and James

Cephas is Aramaic for "Peter." Peter comes from the Greek term *petros*, rock, Cephas from the Aramaic *kepa*, rock. James, the half-brother of Jesus and the son of Mary and Joseph, was a leader of the Jerusalem church. He is also the likely author of the epistle of James.

ONE STEP FURTHER:

Syria

If you have some extra time this week, find out what significant New Testament city was located in Syria. Record it below along with why it was so important.

What does Paul *not* do immediately after his conversion?

What does he do? Where does he go?

Arabia . . . Damascus

Acts 9 tells us that Paul (then called Saul) was on his way to Damascus (northeast of Israel) when he met Jesus. Paul says that after his conversion, he didn't immediately go to the Christian epicenter in Jerusalem, but rather went south to Arabia. Here's a simple map showing the relative locations.

Where are the leaders of the early church primarily located?

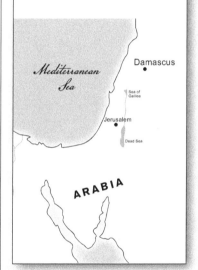

When does Paul finally consult with other Christian leaders? Who are they?

Did the church at large accept Paul? Explain.

Is it significant that he hadn't spent a lot of time in Judea, the region where Jerusalem is located? Why or why not?

Galatians
Solid Truth for Slippery Times

Who received glory from Paul's work? (Remember this for future reference!)

Does your life cause people to glorify God? Why/why not?

@THE END OF THE DAY . . .

Take some extended time to review what you've learned this week in Galatians 1. Then, write a one-phrase chapter title followed by a one- to two-sentence chapter recap. Finally, spend some time asking God what application you need to take from this chapter for your life. Write that down, too, before you call it a day.

Galatians 1

Title:

Recap:

My Application(s):

Week Two
A Cross at the Heart of the True Gospel

I have been crucified with Christ; and it is no longer I who live, but Christ lives in me; and the life *which I now live in the flesh I live by faith in the Son of God, who loved me and gave Himself up for me.*
–Galatians 2:20

The core message of Galatians 2 is crystal clear—a man is justified through faith in Christ Jesus not by the works of the Law. There is a cross at the heart of the Gospel. As we study this week, be aware that chapter 2 also recounts some events in Paul's life that can sidetrack us into details that do not change the chapter's message. When Paul talks about visiting Jerusalem was he referring to the Jerusalem Council of Acts 15 or an earlier visit? Remember that while good scholars divide on the answer, the issue does not change Paul's clear message. Regardless of the timing of events, the truth remains: justification is through faith alone and never by works of the Law.

REMEMBERING

Take a few minutes to summarize what you learned last week.

WEEKLY READ-THROUGH #1

Version I read:

New observations/questions:

WEEKLY READ-THROUGH #2

Version I read:

New observations/questions:

Galatians
Solid Truth for Slippery Times

SETTING the SCENE

Having expressed his amazement at the Galatians' quick turn from the true Gospel in chapter 1, Paul continues the defense of his apostleship and, in turn, the true Gospel he preaches as received from Jesus Christ and confirmed by his fellow apostles.

GALATIANS 2
OBSERVE the TEXT of SCRIPTURE

READ Galatians 2 and **MARK** key, repeated words in a distinctive fashion.

Galatians 2

1   *Then after an interval of fourteen years I went up again to Jerusalem with Barnabas, taking Titus along also.*

2   *It was because of a revelation that I went up; and I submitted to them the gospel which I preach among the Gentiles, but I did so in private to those who were of reputation, for fear that I might be running, or had run, in vain.*

3   *But not even Titus, who was with me, though he was a Greek, was compelled to be circumcised.*

4   *But it was because of the false brethren secretly brought in, who had sneaked in to spy out our liberty which we have in Christ Jesus, in order to bring us into bondage.*

5   *But we did not yield in subjection to them for even an hour, so that the truth of the gospel would remain with you.*

6   *But from those who were of high reputation (what they were makes no difference to me; God shows no partiality)—well, those who were of reputation contributed nothing to me.*

7   *But on the contrary, seeing that I had been entrusted with the gospel to the uncircumcised, just as Peter had been to the circumcised*

8   *(for He who effectually worked for Peter in his apostleship to the circumcised effectually worked for me also to the Gentiles),*

9   *and recognizing the grace that had been given to me, James and Cephas and John, who were reputed to be pillars, gave to me and Barnabas the right hand of fellowship, so that we might go to the Gentiles and they to the circumcised.*

10 *They only asked us to remember the poor—the very thing I also was eager to do.*

11 *But when Cephas came to Antioch, I opposed him to his face, because he stood condemned.*

12 *For prior to the coming of certain men from James, he used to eat with the Gentiles; but when they came, he began to withdraw and hold himself aloof, fearing the party of the circumcision.*

13 *The rest of the Jews joined him in hypocrisy, with the result that even Barnabas was carried away by their hypocrisy.*

MEMORIZE:

Galatians 2:20-21
"I have been crucified with Christ; and it is no longer I who live, but Christ lives in me; and the life which I now live in the flesh I live by faith in the Son of God, who loved me and gave Himself up for me. I do not nullify the grace of God, for if righteousness comes through the Law, then Christ died needlessly."

Galatians
Solid Truth for Slippery Times

14 But when I saw that they were not straightforward about the truth of the gospel, I said to Cephas in the presence of all, "If you, being a Jew, live like the Gentiles and not like the Jews, how is it that you compel the Gentiles to live like Jews?

15 "We are Jews by nature and not sinners from among the Gentiles;

16 nevertheless knowing that a man is not justified by the works of the Law but through faith in Christ Jesus, even we have believed in Christ Jesus, so that we may be justified by faith in Christ and not by the works of the Law; since by the works of the Law no flesh will be justified.

17 "But if, while seeking to be justified in Christ, we ourselves have also been found sinners, is Christ then a minister of sin? May it never be!

18 "For if I rebuild what I have once destroyed, I prove myself to be a transgressor.

19 "For through the Law I died to the Law, so that I might live to God.

20 "I have been crucified with Christ; and it is no longer I who live, but Christ lives in me; and the life which I now live in the flesh I live by faith in the Son of God, who loved me and gave Himself up for me.

21 "I do not nullify the grace of God, for if righteousness comes through the Law, then Christ died needlessly."

DISCUSS with your GROUP or PONDER on your own . . .

What did you initially observe from the text?

What key words did you notice?

Who are the main people Paul mentions in this section?

What main issue does he address?

When did the events he describes happen?

Where did they take place? What cities does Paul talk about and in what context?

Why is the issue of circumcision such a big deal?

What other questions do you have about Galatians 2?

Galatians
Solid Truth for Slippery Times

Digging Deeper

The Meeting in Jerusalem

A sticky question is where the events of Galatians 2 fit in with the events in Acts. Does the meeting Paul and Barnabas attended in Jerusalem according to Galatians 2:1-10 correspond to the one in Acts 11:27-30 (the relief trip) or to the one in Acts 15 (the Jerusalem Council)? If you have some extra time this week, compare each account with the events in Galatians 2 and see what you think. Then spend some time in your commentaries to see how your conclusions hold up.

Key elements recorded in Galatians 2:

How do the events in Galatians 2 align with those in Acts 11:27-30?

High alignment:	Potential problems:

How do the events in Galatians 2 align with those in Acts 15?

High alignment:	Potential problems:

Commentaries on Galatians
One of the better one-volume commentaries on the market today is *The New Bible Commentary* edited by D.A. Carson. For an advanced exegetical commentary check out *The New International Greek Commentary* by F.F. Bruce.

If you have access to commentaries, record your key findings from these.

What do you think? Is Galatians 2 referring to Paul's trip to Jerusalem in Acts 11 or Acts 15? Explain your reasoning.

LOOKING CLOSER . . .
OBSERVE the TEXT of SCRIPTURE

READ Galatians 2:1-10 and **MARK** all references to people, to the gospel, and to reputation.

Galatians 2:1-10

1 Then after an interval of fourteen years I went up again to Jerusalem with Barnabas, taking Titus along also.

2 It was because of a revelation that I went up; and I submitted to them the gospel which I preach among the Gentiles, but I did so in private to those who were of reputation, for fear that I might be running, or had run, in vain.

3 But not even Titus, who was with me, though he was a Greek, was compelled to be circumcised.

4 But it was because of the false brethren secretly brought in, who had sneaked in to spy out our liberty which we have in Christ Jesus, in order to bring us into bondage.

5 But we did not yield in subjection to them for even an hour, so that the truth of the gospel would remain with you.

6 But from those who were of high reputation (what they were makes no difference to me; God shows no partiality)—well, those who were of reputation contributed nothing to me.

7 But on the contrary, seeing that I had been entrusted with the gospel to the uncircumcised, just as Peter had been to the circumcised

8 (for He who effectually worked for Peter in his apostleship to the circumcised effectually worked for me also to the Gentiles),

9 and recognizing the grace that had been given to me, James and Cephas and John, who were reputed to be pillars, gave to me and Barnabas the right hand of fellowship, so that we might go to the Gentiles and they to the circumcised.

10 They only asked us to remember the poor—the very thing I also was eager to do.

DISCUSS with your GROUP or PONDER on your own . . .

What people does Paul mention in this chapter? What categories would you group them into?

Timing

While we can't know with absolute certainty the time Paul refers to in Galatians 2:1-10, we can still frame it within parameters. That Paul and Barnabas traveled together likely puts this trip before the Paul/Barnabas split that took place just prior to the second of Paul's three missionary journeys.

ONE STEP FURTHER:

Word Study: *Dokeo*

If you have some extra time this week, see what you can unearth on the word *dokeo*, translated *reputation*, and other Greek words related to it. Where else does Paul use it? How else is it used in the New Testament? Record your findings below.

Galatians
Solid Truth for Slippery Times

Why did Paul go to Jerusalem and what did he do when he got there?

Was he summoned by church leaders? Why does this matter?

Who accompanied Paul to Jerusalem? What's significant about each person?

How did Titus differ from everyone else?

What does Paul say about the false brethren? What characterizes them?

ONE STEP FURTHER:

Circumcision
Perplexed by the big deal made out of circumcision? Check out Genesis 17 to learn the background of this sign of God's covenant with Israel. Then read Exodus 4:18-26 and Joshua 5:1-12 to see accounts of circumcision in the lives of Moses' sons and of the men entering the Promised Land under Joshua. Record your findings below.

ONE STEP FURTHER:

Barnabas
Barnabas means "son of encouragement." If you have some extra time this week see what else you can learn about Paul's edifying travel companion.

How does their behavior in Galatians 2 compare with what we learned about them in Galatians 1?

ONE STEP FURTHER:

Titus

We know he's one of Paul's traveling companions and we know Paul wrote a letter to him bearing his name. What else can you discover this week about Titus? Run a concordance search on his name and record what you discover below.

What can we learn from Paul's situation regarding false brethren that's applicable today?

Although we're not fighting over circumcision, what subjects reflect legalistic (and therefore spiritual) bondage in our day?

Why does Paul perceive the false brethren to be such a threat?

What do you think are some modern threats to the Gospel?

Based on this text, would you say Paul was submissive to authority? Why or why not?

Who does Paul answer to?

How do Paul's views align with the church leaders' in Jerusalem? What do both parties acknowledge?

Why does Peter go to the Jews and Paul to the Gentiles?

We see in this text that God entrusted the Gospel to and effectively worked for Peter in his apostleship to the Jewish people and Paul in his to the Gentiles. Are you responding to God's call, gifting, and working in your life? Are you making plans accordingly? Explain.

LOOKING CLOSER . . .

In the first half of Galatians 2, Paul recounts a meeting in Jerusalem. Some see this as the relief trip referred to Acts 11 while others think it is the Jerusalem Council of Acts 15. In either case, the point of discussion is the same: the true Gospel. Whether you correlate with Acts 11 or Acts 15, the bottom line remains—Paul preached a Gospel consistent with the Gospel preached by the original apostles and the Jerusalem church and confirmed by them. All agreed that the Gospel should go out to both the circumcised and the uncircumcised, to Jews and Gentiles.

INDUCTIVE FOCUS:

Using Your Own Symbols

Marking the text will help key words stand out visually but the method of **marking** you use (if you choose to **mark** at all) is entirely up to you. You may prefer using colors over symbols or you may prefer upping a font size on an electronic text of Scripture. Whatever you choose, always remember that **marking** is a means to the end of understanding the text and never an end in itself.

OBSERVE the TEXT of SCRIPTURE

READ Galatians 2:11-21 and **MARK** references to each person or group of people in a distinctive fashion. Be especially careful to mark pronouns.

Galatians 2:11-21

11 But when Cephas came to Antioch, I opposed him to his face, because he stood condemned.

12 For prior to the coming of certain men from James, he used to eat with the Gentiles; but when they came, he began to withdraw and hold himself aloof, fearing the party of the circumcision.

13 The rest of the Jews joined him in hypocrisy, with the result that even Barnabas was carried away by their hypocrisy.

14 But when I saw that they were not straightforward about the truth of the gospel, I said to Cephas in the presence of all, "If you, being a Jew, live like the Gentiles and not like the Jews, how is it that you compel the Gentiles to live like Jews?

15 "We are Jews by nature and not sinners from among the Gentiles;

16 nevertheless knowing that a man is not justified by the works of the Law but through faith in Christ Jesus, even we have believed in Christ Jesus, so that we may be justified by faith in Christ and not by the works of the Law; since by the works of the Law no flesh will be justified.

17 "But if, while seeking to be justified in Christ, we ourselves have also been found sinners, is Christ then a minister of sin? May it never be!

18 "For if I rebuild what I have once destroyed, I prove myself to be a transgressor.

19 "For through the Law I died to the Law, so that I might live to God.

20 "I have been crucified with Christ; and it is no longer I who live, but Christ lives in me; and the life which I now live in the flesh I live by faith in the Son of God, who loved me and gave Himself up for me.

21 "I do not nullify the grace of God, for if righteousness comes through the Law, then Christ died needlessly."

DISCUSS with your GROUP or PONDER on your own . . .

Who shows up in this section? What people and people groups appear? How is everyone connected? Where are the differences?

Antecedent

Simply put, an antecedent is a noun further back in a sentence that a pronoun refers back to. Whenever we see a pronoun (*I*, *you*, *he*, *she*, *they*, etc.), we know that it is substituting for a noun. Usually pronouns are understood by context, but in complex sentences, we need to pay close attention to make sure we understand which noun a particular pronoun is replacing. In Galatians 2:11-21, paying close attention to the antecedents *their* and *they* will be very helpful in understanding the passage.

Just by way of review, what other name is Cephas known by? (If you don't remember, check out John 1:42.)

What has Paul already said about his other meetings with Peter? Briefly summarize each.

How would you characterize their relationship based on the text? Was it good? Bad? Tense? Warm? Cool? Why?

Where was "home base" for Cephas?

Word Studies: The Words Describing Peter

If you have some time this week find the Greek words Paul uses with regard to Peter. See where else they are used in the biblical text and what light they shed on this passage. When you've looked at the other usages for yourself, feel free to consult word study helps.

Where was "home base" for Paul?

stood condemned

On whose "turf" does the tussle between Paul and Cephas take place?

began to withdraw

aloof

Briefly describe the events that lead up to Paul squaring off with Cephas.

fearing

On what basis does Paul say that Cephas "stood condemned"?

Digging Deeper

Getting to Know Peter . . . The First and Second Epistles

If you have some extra time this week, read through the two New Testament letters attributed to Peter. See what you can learn about his character at the time he wrote. What issues were on his heart as he wrote? How would you describe the theme or main point of each of his letters?

1 Peter
Theme:
Peter's character:

Peter's message:

2 Peter
Theme:
Peter's character:

Peter's message:

FYI:

Love Covers a Multitude of Sins

Above all, keep fervent in your love for one another, because love covers a multitude of sins.

—1 Peter 4:8

Galatians
Solid Truth for Slippery Times

Have you ever behaved differently because you feared what others might think or how they would react? Explain.

Is shutting up sometimes a wise course of action? When is it and when is it not? Explain your reasoning.

Why was Peter's silence inappropriate in this situation?

What effect did Peter's withdrawal have on those around him?

When was the last time you seriously considered what effect your behavior, words, or lack of words have on others? How has your life influenced others' lives?

Where do you look for cues on how to live? Is there a "right place" to look? Explain your reasoning.

Who at Antioch was guilty of not being "straightforward about the truth of the gospel"?

When Paul calls Peter out, who is around? Based on the text, do you think there is a reason for this?

Is there any indication from this text or anywhere else that Peter contended with him?

From your knowledge of Scripture, was Peter afraid at other times? If so, when? What were the eventual outcomes? (Be sure to cite the references for your answer.)

How do you "know when to hold 'em? Know when to fold 'em?" How do you know when to stand up and be heard? Support your answer from the Word.

ONE STEP FURTHER:

Word Studies:
Again, if you have some time this week, see what you can find out about the words Paul uses with reference to the Jewish believers.

in hypocrisy

not straightforward

Galatians
Solid Truth for Slippery Times

Digging Deeper

Peter in the Gospels

If you have time, take a journey through the Gospels this week to see what kind of picture they paint of Peter. You can read or listen through any or all of the Gospel accounts or you can use a concordance to drill down to the specific texts relating to Peter. Pay close attention to Peter's growth between the time he walked with Jesus and the time he penned his letters.

Matthew

Mark

Luke

John

How does Peter of the Gospels compare with Peter of the Epistles?

LOOKING EVEN CLOSER . . .

We've already read Galatians 2:15-21, but let's move in for a closer look at these densely packed treasures.

OBSERVE the TEXT of SCRIPTURE

READ Galatians 2:15-21 and **MARK** references to *righteousness/justified*, *the Law*, *faith/believe*, *life* and *death*.

Galatians 2:15-21

15 *"We are Jews by nature and not sinners from among the Gentiles;*

16 *nevertheless knowing that a man is not justified by the works of the Law but through faith in Christ Jesus, even we have believed in Christ Jesus, so that we may be justified by faith in Christ and not by the works of the Law; since by the works of the Law no flesh will be justified.*

17 *"But if, while seeking to be justified in Christ, we ourselves have also been found sinners, is Christ then a minister of sin? May it never be!*

18 *"For if I rebuild what I have once destroyed, I prove myself to be a transgressor.*

19 *"For through the Law I died to the Law, so that I might live to God.*

20 *"I have been crucified with Christ; and it is no longer I who live, but Christ lives in me; and the life which I now live in the flesh I live by faith in the Son of God, who loved me and gave Himself up for me.*

21 *"I do not nullify the grace of God, for if righteousness comes through the Law, then Christ died needlessly."*

DISCUSS with your GROUP or PONDER on your own . . .

What does Paul say about justification and righteousness in this section? How can people be justified? What will never work?

What is distinctive about saving faith?

Week Two: **A Cross at the Heart of the True Gospel**

What can't the Law do? According to verse 19 what is one thing it can do?

Righteousness and Justified
Why are we marking *righteousness* and *justified* the same way? Because they come from the same Greek root.

Justified = *dikaioo* (verb)

Righteousness = *dikaiosune* (noun)

How does Paul explain faith in Christ according to verse 20? Be specific.

Faith and Believe
Faith and *believe* also come from a common Greek root.

Faith = *pistis* (noun)

Believe = *pisteuo* (verb)

What exchange takes place? In what sense does the Christian now live?

Does your life reflect this reality? In what ways?

What does this section teach about Christ? (You may want to go back to mark your text one more time and make a simple list.)

FYI:

Crucified with Christ
When Paul says "I have been crucified with Christ" *(christo sunestauromai)* he uses the perfect tense of the Greek verb which indicates a past completed action with a continuous and ongoing result.

If people can work their way to God, what bearing does this have on the sacrifice of Jesus?

@THE END OF THE DAY . . .

Mankind's sin is great. Jesus Christ's sacrifice is greater! As you close out your week of study, ask God to reveal any Law-based behaviors holding you captive. Then, spend some time considering what implications come with living a crucified life. If you need to write something down in response, by all means do so.

It's Always Been Faith

*Are you so foolish? Having begun by the Spirit,
are you now being perfected by the flesh?*
−Galatians 3:3

Paul has gone to great lengths in the opening chapters to establish his apostleship and his Gospel as originating in Christ Himself. The Gospel he preaches is the Gospel church leaders in Jerusalem preach, although he did not receive it from them. Both he and the apostles at Jerusalem received the one and only true Gospel from Jesus Himself and this common Gospel stands in contrast to the false gospel Judaizers have imposed.

As we move into Galatians 3, we'll see that the true Gospel did not change God's mode of operation. The God who saves has always saved on the basis of faith and not works. The Judaizers who were so bound up in following God's Law missed the truth that even before God gave the Law to Moses, Abraham was justified by faith!

Are you remembering to pray?
Jesus tells us in John 16:13 that when the Spirit of truth comes, He will guide us into all the truth. It's important for us to remember to pray that the Holy Spirit will be our Teacher and Guide as we study the Word.

REMEMBERING

Take a few minutes to summarize Galatians 1 and 2. Describe them separately, together, in outline or prose. Use whatever technique helps you remember best and record your thoughts below. As you're summarizing, ask yourself "Would this make sense to someone else if I were telling it to them?"

The Significance of Abraham

It's easy for Gentile believers in Jesus to miss the significance of Abraham and simply lump him in with other Old Testament heroes. His relationship with God, however, stands out because it shows a relationship of faith that pre-dates the Law. God gave the Law to Moses and from that time until the coming of Jesus, the Law provided a structure to relate to God by revealing to people both their sin and their need for a Savior.

God's dealings with Abraham on the basis of faith show that reconciliation to God on the basis of faith is not a new thing. It's the way God has always worked. It's older than Paul and older than Peter and James and even older than the Law itself.

WEEKLY READ-THROUGH #1

Version I read:

New observations/questions:

WEEKLY READ-THROUGH #2

Version I read:

New observations/questions:

Identifying "Contrasts"
One inductive study tool is identifying contrasts in the text. Just before reading Galatians 3 is a great time to pull that tool out of the box. Watch for contrasting pairs in the text and jot them down below.

SETTING the SCENE

Paul has expressed his amazement at the Galatians' turn from the true Gospel in chapter 1 and has affirmed in chapter 2 that a man is justified by faith in Christ Jesus and not by the works of the Law. He also recounted his conflict with Peter over his withdrawal from fellowship with Gentile believers.

GALATIANS 3
OBSERVE the TEXT of SCRIPTURE

READ Galatians 3 and **MARK** key, repeated words in a distinctive fashion. In this section, in particular, watch for contrasting pairs of words and concepts.

Galatians 3

1 *You foolish Galatians, who has bewitched you, before whose eyes Jesus Christ was publicly portrayed as crucified?*

2 *This is the only thing I want to find out from you: did you receive the Spirit by the works of the Law, or by hearing with faith?*

3 *Are you so foolish? Having begun by the Spirit, are you now being perfected by the flesh?*

4 *Did you suffer so many things in vain—if indeed it was in vain?*

Galatians
Solid Truth for Slippery Times

5 So then, does He who provides you with the Spirit and works miracles among you, do it by the works of the Law, or by hearing with faith?

6 Even so Abraham BELIEVED GOD, AND IT WAS RECKONED TO HIM AS RIGHTEOUSNESS.

7 Therefore, be sure that it is those who are of faith who are sons of Abraham.

8 The Scripture, foreseeing that God would justify the Gentiles by faith, preached the gospel beforehand to Abraham, saying, "ALL THE NATIONS WILL BE BLESSED IN YOU."

9 So then those who are of faith are blessed with Abraham, the believer.

10 For as many as are of the works of the Law are under a curse; for it is written, "CURSED IS EVERYONE WHO DOES NOT ABIDE BY ALL THINGS WRITTEN IN THE BOOK OF THE LAW, TO PERFORM THEM."

11 Now that no one is justified by the Law before God is evident; for, "THE RIGHTEOUS MAN SHALL LIVE BY FAITH."

12 However, the Law is not of faith; on the contrary, "HE WHO PRACTICES THEM SHALL LIVE BY THEM."

13 Christ redeemed us from the curse of the Law, having become a curse for us—for it is written, "CURSED IS EVERYONE WHO HANGS ON A TREE"—

14 in order that in Christ Jesus the blessing of Abraham might come to the Gentiles, so that we would receive the promise of the Spirit through faith.

15 Brethren, I speak in terms of human relations: even though it is only a man's covenant, yet when it has been ratified, no one sets it aside or adds conditions to it.

16 Now the promises were spoken to Abraham and to his seed. He does not say, "And to seeds," as referring to many, but rather to one, "And to your seed," that is, Christ.

17 What I am saying is this: the Law, which came four hundred and thirty years later, does not invalidate a covenant previously ratified by God, so as to nullify the promise.

18 For if the inheritance is based on law, it is no longer based on a promise; but God has granted it to Abraham by means of a promise.

19 Why the Law then? It was added because of transgressions, having been ordained through angels by the agency of a mediator, until the seed would come to whom the promise had been made.

20 Now a mediator is not for one party only; whereas God is only one.

21 Is the Law then contrary to the promises of God? May it never be! For if a law had been given which was able to impart life, then righteousness would indeed have been based on law.

22 But the Scripture has shut up everyone under sin, so that the promise by faith in Jesus Christ might be given to those who believe.

23 But before faith came, we were kept in custody under the law, being shut up to the faith which was later to be revealed.

24 Therefore the Law has become our tutor to lead us to Christ, so that we may be justified by faith.

25 *But now that faith has come, we are no longer under a tutor.*

26 *For you are all sons of God through faith in Christ Jesus.*

27 *For all of you who were baptized into Christ have clothed yourselves with Christ.*

28 *There is neither Jew nor Greek, there is neither slave nor free man, there is neither male nor female; for you are all one in Christ Jesus.*

29 *And if you belong to Christ, then you are Abraham's descendants, heirs according to promise.*

DISCUSS with your GROUP or PONDER on your own . . .

How does Galatians 3 fit in with the flow of the letter so far?

What are your initial observations/questions on this chapter?

What repeating word groups and phrases did you notice?

What two ways of living does Paul contrast and what does he say about each?

ONE STEP FURTHER:

Word Study: Foolish

If you have time this week, find the Greek word translated *foolish* in Galatians 3:1 and 3 and see what you can discover about it. Where else is it used? How does it compare to other words translated "foolish" in the New Testament? Record your findings below.

According to Paul, how long have God's sights been set on the Gentiles? Explain from the text.

LOOKING EVEN CLOSER . . .
OBSERVE the TEXT of SCRIPTURE

READ Galatians 3:1-5 and **MARK** references to *the Spirit* and *the flesh*. Also mark the phrases *the works of the Law* and *hearing with faith*.

Galatians 3:1-5

1 You foolish Galatians, who has bewitched you, before whose eyes Jesus Christ was publicly portrayed as crucified?

2 This is the only thing I want to find out from you: did you receive the Spirit by the works of the Law, or by hearing with faith?

3 Are you so foolish? Having begun by the Spirit, are you now·being perfected by the flesh?

4 Did you suffer so many things in vain—if indeed it was in vain?

5 So then, does He who provides you with the Spirit and works miracles among you, do it by the works of the Law, or by hearing with faith?

DISCUSS with your GROUP or PONDER on your own . . .

How many questions does Paul use in this section as he is addresses his readers? What are the basic questions?

Bewitched!

Words that appear only once in the Bible make it more difficult for us to get a good grasp on meaning without going to study aides. Such is the case with *bewitched (baskaino)*. This Greek word draws attention to a couple of other words in the near context. First are the two references to *foolish (anoetos)*, literally "mindless." Second are the two sight references, *eyes (ophthalmos)* in verse 1 and *foreseeing (proorao)* in verse 8.

What response does each question expect?

In ancient Greek works *baskaino* has a sense of hurting someone with a look, *casting an evil eye*. While there is no real "magic" involved, the word shows the power of a lie to cause people who have seen with their eyes and know better to behave as though they have no minds at all and as though they have seen and know nothing.

What contrast does Paul make between the Spirit and the flesh?

Similarly, what contrast does he make between the phrases "the works of the Law" and "hearing with faith"?

Paul's question to the Galatians is equally applicable today: *Did you receive the Spirit by the works of the Law, or by hearing with faith?* Are there ways that you are trying to be perfected by the flesh? If so, how?

Solid Truth for Slippery Times

Week Three: **It's Always Been Faith**

Judaizers tried to "perfect" themselves by the flesh and taught others to do so. Have you seen modern instances of this teaching? Explain.

How do "works of the Law" differ from the "works" in Ephesians 2:8-10?

How does God perfect us according to the text? Is there anything about this that seems to pose practical problems? If so, explain.

Do you see the difference between perfecting yourself and God perfecting you? Can you give some examples from your own life?

Is lethargy a possible threat to the perfection God calls us to if we don't try to perfect *OURSELVES*? Explain your answer carefully from Scripture.

Digging Deeper

Abraham and the Covenant of Promise

If you have some extra time this week, you'll find that exploring the Old Testament background of Genesis 15 will help dramatically in understanding Paul's argument in the latter half of Galatians 3. Read Galatians 3, then follow up by reading Genesis 15 to see how the two compare.

What Paul says about Abraham in Galatians 3:

How this compares with Genesis 15:

Summary:

LOOKING EVEN CLOSER . . .
OBSERVE the TEXT of SCRIPTURE

READ Galatians 3:6-14 and **MARK** references to *belief/faith* and *justify/righteous(ness)*. There are other key words in this section that you can mark, but the text will get messy fast as there are so many significant, repeating words in these verses.

Galatians 3:6-14

6 *Even so Abraham BELIEVED GOD, AND IT WAS RECKONED TO HIM AS RIGHTEOUSNESS.*

7 *Therefore, be sure that it is those who are of faith who are sons of Abraham.*

8 *The Scripture, foreseeing that God would justify the Gentiles by faith, preached the gospel beforehand to Abraham, saying, "ALL THE NATIONS WILL BE BLESSED IN YOU."*

9 *So then those who are of faith are blessed with Abraham, the believer.*

10 *For as many as are of the works of the Law are under a curse; for it is written, "CURSED IS EVERYONE WHO DOES NOT ABIDE BY ALL THINGS WRITTEN IN THE BOOK OF THE LAW, TO PERFORM THEM."*

11 *Now that no one is justified by the Law before God is evident; for, "THE RIGHTEOUS MAN SHALL LIVE BY FAITH."*

12 *However, the Law is not of faith; on the contrary, "HE WHO PRACTICES THEM SHALL LIVE BY THEM."*

13 *Christ redeemed us from the curse of the Law, having become a curse for us—for it is written, "CURSED IS EVERYONE WHO HANGS ON A TREE"—*

14 *in order that in Christ Jesus the blessing of Abraham might come to the Gentiles, so that we would receive the promise of the Spirit through faith.*

DISCUSS with your GROUP or PONDER on your own . . .

Make a simple list of everything the text says about Abraham.

Why did God declare Abraham righteous? Was it on the basis of something he did? How do you know?

Galatians
Solid Truth for Slippery Times

How was the Gospel preached beforehand to Abraham?

How is God's accounting Abraham's faith to be righteousness significant to Paul's argument?

Consider for a moment the different people and groups mentioned in this letter. Which of them would naturally claim Abraham as their father?

Who does Paul say are "sons of Abraham"? How does sonship benefit them? What does this mean to their current situation?

What different life paths is Paul describing? How does he contrast them?

FYI:

Abraham Believed God in Romans, too!

Paul quotes the Genesis account in Romans while making the point that Abraham was justified by faith prior to the giving of the Law.

What then shall we say that Abraham, our forefather according to the flesh, has found? For if Abraham was justified by works, he has something to boast about, but not before God. For what does the Scripture say? "ABRAHAM BELIEVED GOD, AND IT WAS CREDITED TO HIM AS RIGHTEOUSNESS."

—Romans 4:1-3

Galatians
Solid Truth for Slippery Times

What does the Law bring to those who are under it? Why?

The Gospel Preached to Abraham

Long before the giving of the Law, God promised to bless the nations through Abraham.

"And I will bless those who bless you, and the one who curses you I will curse. And in you all the families of the earth will be blessed."

—Genesis 12:3

How does the negative function of the Law drive man to justification by faith?

Make a simple list of everything the text says about *faith/belief*.

Has there ever been a time when God did not work on the basis of faith? Explain your answer from the text.

What truth about *faith/belief* has been most significant in your life?

According to Galatians 3:11, how does the righteous man live? Where is Paul quoting from? What does he mean by this statement?

Does your life evidence justification by faith or works? Explain.

Thinking from the standpoint of a first century Jewish believer, how new was the Gentile mission compared to historic Judaism? According to this text, how long had the Gentiles been a part of God's plan?

ONE STEP FURTHER:

Reason From Scripture

If you're up for a jaunt through the Scriptures this week, consider the following questions and reason through them from Scripture. Should the Jews have preached their prophecies of the Messiah and His kingdom to the Gentiles in Old Testament times? Why or why not? Is there any evidence that they did? Record your findings below.

Galatians
Solid Truth for Slippery Times

Digging Deeper

A God Who Seeks the Nations

If you have some extra time this week, consider the missionary God we serve. Who are some notable "saved"s among the nations? Think through biblical history—the "truthline" of Scripture—and record some of the notable Gentiles that God graciously grafted into His people. You can do this by section of the Bible, by nations, or by some other way. Briefly recount how God brought each of these people into relationship with Himself.

ONE STEP FURTHER:

Examine the Quoted Texts

Take some extra time this week to explore the contexts of the other Old Testament passages Paul quotes in the text. We've already seen the Genesis quotes on the previous pages. Paul also quotes twice from Deuteronomy and once each from Habakkuk and Leviticus. Find the original references and explore the quotes in their original contexts. Then record your observations below.

LOOKING EVEN CLOSER . . .
OBSERVE the TEXT of SCRIPTURE

READ Galatians 3:15-29 and **MARK** references *promise, seed,* and *Christ.* Keep watching for *faith* and *Law,* but use discretion in marking as the text will clutter quickly.

Galatians 3:15-29

15   *Brethren, I speak in terms of human relations: even though it is only a man's covenant, yet when it has been ratified, no one sets it aside or adds conditions to it.*

16   *Now the promises were spoken to Abraham and to his seed. He does not say, "And to seeds," as referring to many, but rather to one, "And to your seed," that is, Christ.*

17   *What I am saying is this: the Law, which came four hundred and thirty years later, does not invalidate a covenant previously ratified by God, so as to nullify the promise.*

18   *For if the inheritance is based on law, it is no longer based on a promise; but God has granted it to Abraham by means of a promise.*

19   *Why the Law then? It was added because of transgressions, having been ordained through angels by the agency of a mediator, until the seed would come to whom the promise had been made.*

20   *Now a mediator is not for one party only; whereas God is only one.*

21   *Is the Law then contrary to the promises of God? May it never be! For if a law had been given which was able to impart life, then righteousness would indeed have been based on law.*

22   *But the Scripture has shut up everyone under sin, so that the promise by faith in Jesus Christ might be given to those who believe.*

23   *But before faith came, we were kept in custody under the law, being shut up to the faith which was later to be revealed.*

24   *Therefore the Law has become our tutor to lead us to Christ, so that we may be justified by faith.*

25   *But now that faith has come, we are no longer under a tutor.*

26   *For you are all sons of God through faith in Christ Jesus.*

27   *For all of you who were baptized into Christ have clothed yourselves with Christ.*

28   *There is neither Jew nor Greek, there is neither slave nor free man, there is neither male nor female; for you are all one in Christ Jesus.*

29   *And if you belong to Christ, then you are Abraham's descendants, heirs according to promise.*

Galatians
Solid Truth for Slippery Times

DISCUSS with your GROUP or PONDER on your own . . .

What are some common characteristics of covenants?

Once a covenant has been ratified, can it be undone or changed? Why or why not?

What did God promise to Abraham? List everything the text tells us about the promise.

When did God's promise to Abraham take place in relation to the giving of the Law? Did the Law undo the promise? Can it? Explain.

Why is this important to Paul's argument?

If the inheritance is based on a promise given prior to the Law and is still in effect after the Law, why have the Law at all? What is the Law's purpose?

Is there still a need for the Law after faith has come? Explain your answer.

What illustration does Paul use to explain how the Law functions?

Make a simple list of everything the text says about faith and Law. How does Paul compare the two? What other words does he bring into the mix?

What benefits belong to those who are "in Christ Jesus"?

How does being "in Christ Jesus" relate us to one another?

Digging Deeper

Neither Jew nor Greek, Neither Slave nor Free, Neither Male nor Female

The first two are clear enough. The third has been controversial. If you have some time this week, see what else the New Testament has to say about the relationship between men and women in the body of Christ. Be sure to investigate the following passages:

Galatians 3:28

1 Corinthians 14:34ff

1 Timothy 2:12ff

Other relevant passages:

My conclusion:

@THE END OF THE DAY . . .

Galatians is a densely packed treasure chest. What truth from the letter has been most precious to you this week?

How are you doing at living in the reality of the cross?

Galatians
Solid Truth for Slippery Times

Week Four
Slave or Son?

*Because you are sons, God has sent forth the Spirit of His Son
into our hearts, crying, "Abba! Father!"*
–Galatians 4:6

Why would anyone choose slavery when God offers sonship? Although illogical, Paul tells us this is exactly what some Jewish believers were leaning into. Rather than choosing to live in the reality and power of the indwelling Spirit of the risen Christ, their ears were open to the call of the Law. They were being drawn back toward the very things Christ had freed them from—not unlike us who are often tempted to do so today!

Old Testament Backgrounds

One of the reasons the Old Testament is so critical is that it provides background for everything that happens in the New Testament. We can't fully understand grace if we don't understand the standards of the Law. This week we'll see another allusion to Abraham and his sons Isaac and Ishmael.

Solid Truth for Slippery Times

REMEMBERING

Take a few minutes to summarize Galatians 1–3.

FYI:

Why the continued reading?

The only way you'll master the book of Galatians is by reading, re-reading and studying it. The workbook will help you but the Book itself is the key. Never, ever let any workbook trump The Book!

WEEKLY READ-THROUGH #1

Version I read:

New observations/questions:

WEEKLY READ-THROUGH #2

Version I read:

New observations/questions:

ONE STEP FURTHER:

Genesis 15–22
If you have some extra time this week, read the initial account of Abraham and his two sons in the book of Genesis. Record your observations below.

SETTING the SCENE

Paul's cool greeting and amazement at the Galatians' turn from the true Gospel in Galatians 1 sets the stage for one of his more theologically charged letters. In Galatians 2 he stands on the bedrock truth that a man is justified by faith in Christ Jesus, never by the works of the Law, and in Galatians 3 he shows that a man is sanctified by faith as well. The Law did not nullify God's promise to Abraham which preceded it. Rather, it became a tutor to lead people to Christ.

GALATIANS 4
OBSERVE the TEXT of SCRIPTURE

READ Galatians 4 and **MARK** key, repeated words in a distinctive fashion.

Galatians 4

1   Now I say, as long as the heir is a child, he does not differ at all from a slave although he is owner of everything,

2   but he is under guardians and managers until the date set by the father.

3   So also we, while we were children, were held in bondage under the elemental things of the world.

4   But when the fullness of the time came, God sent forth His Son, born of a woman, born under the Law,

5   so that He might redeem those who were under the Law, that we might receive the adoption as sons.

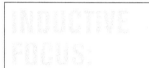

Doing Your Own Word Study
Doing your own word study involves more than just looking up a word in a Bible dictionary or word study tool. Although these tools are important, the groundwork for a word study involves using a concordance to locate every occurrence of the word and its related word-group members in the text of Scripture and checking them out in context. Running to a word study book first is like running to a commentary before reading the text of Scripture—it's a big "no no."

6 *Because you are sons, God has sent forth the Spirit of His Son into our hearts, crying, "Abba! Father!"*

7 *Therefore you are no longer a slave, but a son; and if a son, then an heir through God.*

8 *However at that time, when you did not know God, you were slaves to those which by nature are no gods.*

9 *But now that you have come to know God, or rather to be known by God, how is it that you turn back again to the weak and worthless elemental things, to which you desire to be enslaved all over again?*

10 *You observe days and months and seasons and years.*

11 *I fear for you, that perhaps I have labored over you in vain.*

12 *I beg of you, brethren, become as I am, for I also have become as you are. You have done me no wrong;*

13 *but you know that it was because of a bodily illness that I preached the gospel to you the first time;*

14 *and that which was a trial to you in my bodily condition you did not despise or loathe, but you received me as an angel of God, as Christ Jesus Himself.*

15 *Where then is that sense of blessing you had? For I bear you witness that, if possible, you would have plucked out your eyes and given them to me.*

16 *So have I become your enemy by telling you the truth?*

17 *They eagerly seek you, not commendably, but they wish to shut you out so that you will seek them.*

18 *But it is good always to be eagerly sought in a commendable manner, and not only when I am present with you.*

19 *My children, with whom I am again in labor until Christ is formed in you—*

20 *but I could wish to be present with you now and to change my tone, for I am perplexed about you.*

21 *Tell me, you who want to be under law, do you not listen to the law?*

22 *For it is written that Abraham had two sons, one by the bondwoman and one by the free woman.*

23 *But the son by the bondwoman was born according to the flesh, and the son by the free woman through the promise.*

24 *This is allegorically speaking, for these women are two covenants: one proceeding from Mount Sinai bearing children who are to be slaves; she is Hagar.*

25 *Now this Hagar is Mount Sinai in Arabia and corresponds to the present Jerusalem, for she is in slavery with her children.*

26 *But the Jerusalem above is free; she is our mother.*

27 *For it is written,*

"REJOICE, BARREN WOMAN WHO DOES NOT BEAR;

BREAK FORTH AND SHOUT, YOU WHO ARE NOT IN LABOR;

Galatians
Solid Truth for Slippery Times

FOR MORE NUMEROUS ARE THE CHILDREN OF THE DESOLATE

THAN OF THE ONE WHO HAS A HUSBAND."

28 *And you brethren, like Isaac, are children of promise.*

29 *But as at that time he who was born according to the flesh persecuted him who was born according to the Spirit, so it is now also.*

30 *But what does the Scripture say?*

"CAST OUT THE BONDWOMAN AND HER SON,

FOR THE SON OF THE BONDWOMAN SHALL NOT BE AN HEIR WITH THE SON OF THE FREE WOMAN."

31 *So then, brethren, we are not children of a bondwoman, but of the free woman.*

DISCUSS with your GROUP or PONDER on your own . . .

What are your initial observations on / questions for this chapter?

What repeating word groups and phrases did you notice in this chapter?

INDUCTIVE FOCUS:

Contrasts and Comparisons
Identifying contrasts and comparisons is an important part of observing the text of Scripture. Galatians 4 is a perfect text for practicing this skill.

Here are a couple of examples to get you started:

Comparisons:
child heir is like a *slave* (4:1)

Contrasts:
son and *slave* (4:7)

Galatians
Solid Truth for Slippery Times

How does Galatians 4 tie in with Galatians 3?

Uninspired Chapter Breaks
The words of Scripture are inspired, the chapter breaks are not. Although we're looking at Galatians chapter by chapter, do note that a significant train of thought runs through Galatians 3 and 4.

What words (or word groups) are contrasts?

What main truth does Paul open the chapter with?

How does this relate to his overall argument?

What fear does Paul express regarding the Galatians? What is it based on?

How has his relationship with them changed over time? What or who was behind this shift?

What Jewish illustration does he use at the end of the chapter? What basic point is he driving at?

From what you've read so far, how would you summarize this chapter in one phrase?

> **INDUCTIVE FOCUS:**
>
> **Marking Time Phrases**
> Observing and marking time phrases also helps us understand the text we're reading. Watch for words like *now, before, after, then, time,* and other time-related words and mark them in a consistent fashion.

LOOKING EVEN CLOSER . . .
OBSERVE the TEXT of SCRIPTURE

READ Galatians 4:1-7 and **MARK** references to *child/son*, *slave*, and all references to *God*.

Galatians 4:1-7

1   Now I say, as long as the heir is a child, he does not differ at all from a slave although he is owner of everything,

2   but he is under guardians and managers until the date set by the father.

3   So also we, while we were children, were held in bondage under the elemental things of the world.

4   But when the fullness of the time came, God sent forth His Son, born of a woman, born under the Law,

5   so that He might redeem those who were under the Law, that we might receive the adoption as sons.

Galatians
Solid Truth for Slippery Times

6 *Because you are sons, God has sent forth the Spirit of His Son into our hearts, crying, "Abba! Father!"*

7 *Therefore you are no longer a slave, but a son; and if a son, then an heir through God.*

Cross-Referencing "Elemental Things"

See to it that no one takes you captive through philosophy and empty deception, according to the tradition of men, according to the **elementary principles** (**stoicheia**) *of the world, rather than according to Christ.*

—Colossians 2:8

DISCUSS with your GROUP or PONDER on your own . . .

What two groups of people have striking similarities? How are they similar? How do they differ?

What other people groups does Paul mention in 3:26-4:7? What are people before they're sons? How do these conditions lead them to becoming sons?

From a Jewish viewpoint, what makes a son of Abraham?

What has Paul already said about sons in Galatians 3? How does one become a son according to 3:26-29?

What time phrases did you notice in 4:1-7? How do they help frame the argument?

Galatians
Solid Truth for Slippery Times

What does Paul mean by "children" in 4:3? What are the possibilities? Support your conclusion from the text.

What was their condition before "receiv[ing] the adoption of sons"?

FYI:

More Elemental Things
If you have died with Christ to the **elementary principles (*stoichieon*)** *of the world, why, as if you were living in the world, do you submit yourself to decrees, such as, "Do not handle, do not taste, do not touch!" (which all* refer *to things destined to perish with use)—in accordance with the commandments and teachings of men?*

—Colossians 2:20-22

What does the text say about the "elemental things"? (Don't worry, we'll look at this more later in the lesson.)

How did things change in the "fullness of time"?

According to Paul, how do people become sons of God? Is anyone naturally born into it? Explain.

What is the Law's place in relation to the work of God's Son?

What changes come with being adopted?

How does adoption characterize our relationship with God?

What has God sent us because we're sons? What difference does this make?

Do you live in light of this reality? If so, how does this truth change the way you think and act on a daily basis?

What implications come with moving from the status of slave to son?

Galatians
Solid Truth for Slippery Times

Notes

Digging Deeper

Examining the Trinity in Galatians

In Galatians 4:6, Paul makes a comment referencing the three members of the Trinity saying, "Because you are sons, God has sent forth the Spirit of His Son into our hearts, crying, 'Abba! Father!'"

What do we learn about the Father in Galatians?

What do we learn about the Son?

What do we learn about the Spirit?

Summarize Paul's use of Trinitarian language in Galatians.

Galatians
Solid Truth for Slippery Times

LOOKING EVEN CLOSER . . .
OBSERVE the TEXT of SCRIPTURE

READ Galatians 4:8-11. In Galatians 4:3 Paul says, "So also we, while we were children, were held in bondage under the **elemental things** of the world." In this section of the text, **MARK** the other occurrence of *elemental things* as well as any synonyms or descriptions of elemental things. Also **MARK** occurrences of *know/ known*.

Galatians 4:8-11

8   However at that time, when you did not know God, you were slaves to those which by nature are no gods.

9   But now that you have come to know God, or rather to be known by God, how is it that you turn back again to the weak and worthless elemental things, to which you desire to be enslaved all over again?

10   You observe days and months and seasons and years.

11   I fear for you, that perhaps I have labored over you in vain.

DISCUSS with your GROUP or PONDER on your own . . .

What phrases did you mark as synonyms and descriptions of *elemental things*?

While *elemental things* is a little cryptic, what does Paul clearly tell us about them? What other phrases or adjectives are paired up with the term? What characterizes slavery to them? Read the text carefully and record your observations.

Galatians
Solid Truth for Slippery Times

Notes

Are you enslaved to any extra-biblical behaviors that others told you would cause spiritual growth but have not? Explain.

Have others tried to force "religious" behaviors on you? In what context? How did you respond?

Are there days, months, seasons, and years that you religiously observe? If so, how is it working for you? How would you defend it? Explain.

What does Paul say about "knowing God"? What is man's condition apart from knowledge of God? How do we come to know God?

Do you ever find yourself desiring methods more than you desire God? What is the remedy?

ONE STEP FURTHER:

Word Study: Know/Known

If you have time, look at the two different words Paul uses in this section of the text for *know/known*. Find out where else they're used in Scripture and how. Then record your findings below.

Galatians
Solid Truth for Slippery Times

What does Paul fear? Do you think his fear is legitimate? Is it possible that his readers are not truly in Christ? Explain.

LOOKING EVEN CLOSER . . .
OBSERVE the TEXT of SCRIPTURE

READ Galatians 4:12-16 paying close attention to the historical context.

Galatians 4:12-16

12 I beg of you, brethren, become as I am, for I also have become as you are. You have done me no wrong;

13 but you know that it was because of a bodily illness that I preached the gospel to you the first time;

14 and that which was a trial to you in my bodily condition you did not despise or loathe, but you received me as an angel of God, as Christ Jesus Himself.

15 Where then is that sense of blessing you had? For I bear you witness that, if possible, you would have plucked out your eyes and given them to me.

16 So have I become your enemy by telling you the truth?

DISCUSS with your GROUP or PONDER on your own . . .

What does Paul earnestly request in verse 12?

How has Paul become like Gentile believers? (Think through his main point in the letter as you answer.)

What can we reconstruct? What don't we know? What can we know clearly?

How has the relationship between Paul and this church changed? What characterized it at first?

FYI:

The Greek Imperative
Paul's exhortation for his readers to "become as I am" (Galatians 4:12) is his first use of the imperative mood (the mood of command) in the letter. He will shift to more specific instruction as the letter progresses.

How did the people treat him before?

What does he fear is happening now? Why?

Have you ever become a person's enemy by telling them the truth?

What challenges do we face when we declare biblical truth?

Galatians
Solid Truth for Slippery Times

Digging Deeper

Truth Telling in a Lying Culture

God's Word says a tremendous amount about truth and lies. This week, see what you can discover on your own about how God's people are to live in the midst of a culture of lies. Respond to these questions based on your study of Scripture.

Based on God's Word, what can we expect from our culture?

What is our responsibility in the face of this?

How should we live as truth tellers? What are some external behaviors that signal this internal reality?

What is the potential cost? Are you willing to pay the price?

LOOKING EVEN CLOSER . . .
OBSERVE the TEXT of SCRIPTURE

READ Galatians 4:17-20 and **MARK** references to *seeking* and to *good/commendable* (same Greek root).

Galatians 4:17-20

17 *They eagerly seek you, not commendably, but they wish to shut you out so that you will seek them.*

18 *But it is good always to be eagerly sought in a commendable manner, and not only when I am present with you.*

19 *My children, with whom I am again in labor until Christ is formed in you—*

20 *but I could wish to be present with you now and to change my tone, for I am perplexed about you.*

DISCUSS with your GROUP or PONDER on your own . . .

Who is eagerly seeking the Gentile believers? For what purpose? (Keep an eye on your key words as you answer.)

What terms of endearment does Paul use in this section?

Describe the emotional tone of this section. Has it changed from previous chapters? How?

Galatians
Solid Truth for Slippery Times

How does Paul's purpose for believers in Galatia differ from the Judaizer's purpose for them?

Word Study: Eagerly Seek
If you have some extra time this week, find the Greek word behind *eagerly seek* and *seek* in Galatians 4:17-18. Where else is the term used in the New Testament and how? Record your findings and takeaways below.

How does Paul describe his condition? Have you ever felt the same way? Explain.

LOOKING EVEN CLOSER . . .
OBSERVE the TEXT of SCRIPTURE

READ Galatians 4:21-31 and **MARK** references to *child/son*, *slave*, and all references to *God*.

Galatians 4:21-31

21 Tell me, you who want to be under law, do you not listen to the law?

22 For it is written that Abraham had two sons, one by the bondwoman and one by the free woman.

23 But the son by the bondwoman was born according to the flesh, and the son by the free woman through the promise.

24 This is allegorically speaking, for these women are two covenants: one proceeding from Mount Sinai bearing children who are to be slaves; she is Hagar.

25 Now this Hagar is Mount Sinai in Arabia and corresponds to the present Jerusalem, for she is in slavery with her children.

26 But the Jerusalem above is free; she is our mother.

27 For it is written,

"REJOICE, BARREN WOMAN WHO DOES NOT BEAR;

BREAK FORTH AND SHOUT, YOU WHO ARE NOT IN LABOR;

FOR MORE NUMEROUS ARE THE CHILDREN OF THE DESOLATE

THAN OF THE ONE WHO HAS A HUSBAND."

28 And you brethren, like Isaac, are children of promise.

Galatians
Solid Truth for Slippery Times

ONE STEP FURTHER:

29 But as at that time he who was born according to the flesh persecuted him who was born *according to the Spirit,* so it is now also.

30 But what does the Scripture say?

"CAST OUT THE BONDWOMAN AND HER SON,

FOR THE SON OF THE BONDWOMAN SHALL NOT BE AN HEIR WITH THE SON OF THE FREE WOMAN."

31 So then, brethren, we are not children of a bondwoman, but of the free woman.

DISCUSS with your GROUP or PONDER on your own . . .

How does Paul address his readers in verse 21? What characterizes them?

What does the Law teach about the differences between the sons of the bondwoman and the free woman?

According to the Law itself, is it better to be "under the Law" or not?

Even Paul was Perplexed

If the Apostle Paul who saw the risen Christ was perplexed, we can know that difficult situations don't just follow us. They've always been around and they'll always be around until Jesus returns. God provided wisdom for Paul and, as James tells us, He will provide wisdom for us as well if we ask for it in faith (James 1:5-6).

All Things to All Men

To the Jews I became as a Jew, so that I might win Jews; to those who are under the Law, as under the Law though not being myself under the Law, so that I might win those who are under the Law; to those who are without law, as without law, though not being without the law of God but under the law of Christ, so that I might win those who are without law. To the weak I became weak, that I might win the weak; I have become all things to all men, so that I may by all means save some. I do all things for the sake of the gospel, so that I may become a fellow partaker of it.

—1 Corinthians 9:20-23

Galatians
Solid Truth for Slippery Times

Let's unpack this by looking at the two categories the Law talks about: the bond-woman and the free woman. Make a simple list showing what is associated with each:

Bondwoman	Free Woman

Which son would Paul's Jewish readers gravitate toward, Isaac or Ishmael?

Describe a basic Jewish understanding of Isaac and Ishmael and their respective offspring.

How did first century Judaism view the Law and what it accomplished?

How does Paul flip the Jews' traditional understanding of the Law upside down? What are the implications? For them? For us?

@THE END OF THE DAY . . .

As you close out your day of study, spend some time considering what it means to live as a son of the free woman. Ask God to help you live in the light of the truth of your freedom in Christ and to reveal to you if there are any ways in your life that do not reflect His freedom. If He brings specific areas to mind, you may want to jot them down below. As we'll see next week, "It was for freedom that Christ set us free!"

Week Five
Set Free for Freedom

*It was for freedom that Christ set us free; therefore keep
standing firm and do not be subject again to a yoke of slavery.*
–Galatians 5:1

Jesus Christ didn't die for us to go running back to slavery–to the Law. He died to
free us so that we would live not for ourselves or for others but for Him. And yet we
still live in human bodies. We still live on a battlefield where the flesh wars against
the Spirit and the Spirit against the flesh. It is on this battlefield that we are called
to keep on standing firm in the freedom that is ours in Christ as men and women
bought with a price.

Bought with a Price
*Or do you not know that your body is a
temple of the Holy Spirit who is in you,
whom you have from God, and that you
are not your own? For you have been
bought with a price: therefore glorify God
in your body.*

–1 Corinthians 6:19-20

REMEMBERING

Take a few minutes to summarize Galatians 1–4.

WEEKLY READ-THROUGH #1

Version I read:

New observations/questions:

WEEKLY READ-THROUGH #2

Version I read:

New observations/questions:

SETTING the SCENE

Having just discussed sonship versus slavery and the contrast between the child of the free woman and the child of the bondwoman in Galatians 4, Paul shifts to applying this freedom lesson in Galatians 5.

GALATIANS 5
OBSERVE the TEXT of SCRIPTURE

READ Galatians 5 and **MARK** key, repeated words in a distinctive fashion.

Galatians 5

1 It was for freedom that Christ set us free; therefore keep standing firm and do not be subject again to a yoke of slavery.

2 Behold I, Paul, say to you that if you receive circumcision, Christ will be of no benefit to you.

3 And I testify again to every man who receives circumcision, that he is under obligation to keep the whole Law.

4 You have been severed from Christ, you who are seeking to be justified by law; you have fallen from grace.

5 For we through the Spirit, by faith, are waiting for the hope of righteousness.

6 For in Christ Jesus neither circumcision nor uncircumcision means anything, but faith working through love.

7 You were running well; who hindered you from obeying the truth?

8 This persuasion did not come from Him who calls you.

9 A little leaven leavens the whole lump of dough.

10 I have confidence in you in the Lord that you will adopt no other view; but the one who is disturbing you will bear his judgment, whoever he is.

11 But I, brethren, if I still preach circumcision, why am I still persecuted? Then the stumbling block of the cross has been abolished.

12 I wish that those who are troubling you would even mutilate themselves.

13 For you were called to freedom, brethren; only do not turn your freedom into an opportunity for the flesh, but through love serve one another.

14 For the whole Law is fulfilled in one word, in the statement, "YOU SHALL LOVE YOUR NEIGHBOR AS YOURSELF."

15 But if you bite and devour one another, take care that you are not consumed by one another.

16 But I say, walk by the Spirit, and you will not carry out the desire of the flesh.

17 For the flesh sets its desire against the Spirit, and the Spirit against the flesh; for these are in opposition to one another, so that you may not do the things that you please.

18 But if you are led by the Spirit, you are not under the Law.

19 *Now the deeds of the flesh are evident, which are: immorality, impurity, sensuality,*

20 *idolatry, sorcery, enmities, strife, jealousy, outbursts of anger, disputes, dissensions, factions,*

21 *envying, drunkenness, carousing, and things like these, of which I forewarn you, just as I have forewarned you, that those who practice such things will not inherit the kingdom of God.*

22 *But the fruit of the Spirit is love, joy, peace, patience, kindness, goodness, faithfulness,*

23 *gentleness, self-control; against such things there is no law.*

24 *Now those who belong to Christ Jesus have crucified the flesh with its passions and desires.*

25 *If we live by the Spirit, let us also walk by the Spirit.*

26 *Let us not become boastful, challenging one another, envying one another.*

DISCUSS with your GROUP or PONDER on your own . . .

How does Galatians 5 tie in with Galatians 4 and the preceding chapters?

What key words did you notice?

What does Paul contrast in this chapter?

What does Paul command in Galatians 5?

Explain Paul's train of thought as he moves through Galatians 5.

LOOKING EVEN CLOSER . . .

Verses never stand alone (they're always in contexts) but Galatians 5:1 is definitely a headliner!!!

OBSERVE the TEXT of SCRIPTURE

READ Galatians 5:1 and **MARK** references to *freedom* and *slavery*.

Galatians 5:1

1 *It was for freedom that Christ set us free; therefore keep standing firm and do not be subject again to a yoke of slavery.*

DISCUSS with your GROUP or PONDER on your own . . .

Has Paul's tone changed from that in the previous section? If so, how?

Who set us free?

A Yoke the Jews Couldn't Bear

The idea of a yoke sounds foreign to many modern readers, but it was common in the first century. In Acts 15:10, Peter refers to the Law as a yoke that the Jewish people could not bear: "Now therefore why do you put God to the test by placing upon the neck of the disciples a yoke which neither our fathers nor we have been able to bear?"

Jesus, by contrast, says in Matthew 11:29-30 that His yoke is easy: "Take My yoke upon you and learn from Me, for I am gentle and humble in heart, and YOU WILL FIND REST FOR YOUR SOULS. For My yoke is easy and My burden is light."

From what and for what are we freed?

What is the proper response to what Christ has done for us? What does Paul call us to do and not do?

Does this contrast with any behavior we've seen so far in this book? Explain.

On a practical note, what concerns might come up from "freedom"? Doesn't "freedom" itself require the *possibility* of evil? Doesn't it, then, open up a world of trouble? Explain.

LOOKING EVEN CLOSER . . .
OBSERVE the TEXT of SCRIPTURE

READ Galatians 5:2-6 and **MARK** references to *justified/righteousness* and *circumcision.*

Galatians 5:2-6

2 Behold I, Paul, say to you that if you receive circumcision, Christ will be of no benefit to you.

3 And I testify again to every man who receives circumcision, that he is under obligation to keep the whole Law.

4 You have been severed from Christ, you who are seeking to be justified by law; you have fallen from grace.

5 For we through the Spirit, by faith, are waiting for the hope of righteousness.

6 For in Christ Jesus neither circumcision nor uncircumcision means anything, but faith working through love.

DISCUSS with your GROUP or PONDER on your own . . .

Who does Paul address specifically in verse 2?

What liability comes with circumcision?

What core issue is at stake? Is it circumcision or something else?

What unexpected result will people who try to work their way to Christ discover in the end? What does believing "circumcision justifies" imply about a person's relationship with the Law and with Christ? Is there any middle ground here?

ONE STEP FURTHER:

Greek Tenses
See what you can discover about the Greek *present* tense this week. What ramifications does its usage have? How does it differ the *aorist* and *perfect* tenses? Record your findings below.

Galatians
Solid Truth for Slippery Times

How is a person justified (declared righteous)?

What does Paul say about faith in verses 5-6? Specifically compare what we are doing in verse 5 with what faith is doing in verse 6.

What does Paul say really matters?

What characterizes the faith Paul proclaims? Why is this important? Why does it matter in our cultural context?

Are you pursuing God by faith or are you trying to work your way to Him? Consider this carefully before you answer.

What hints that a person may be depending on works to make himself right with God?

Can we differentiate behavior that reflects faith in God's righteousness from behavior that reflects faith in works? If so, how?

Digging Deeper

Freedom

If you have some extra time this week, explore the concept of freedom throughout the Bible. In order to do this, you'll want to consider times when people and nations lost their freedom and when they regained it, as well as what Jesus and biblical authors have to say about freedom. Here are a few questions to get you started.

What instances of slavery does the Old Testament recount? Consider first, people who were enslaved.

What about corporate slavery? (Consider both the Jewish people and other nations.) How many years of slavery had the Jews endured throughout biblical history? (Can you add them up?) Then, by contrast, how many years of relative freedom did they have and when (e.g., during whose reigns)? (This will take some doing if you're up to it.)

What does Jesus say about freedom?

What do other New Testament writers say?

Summary:

FYI:

As Far Back as Genesis
In Romans 4:3-5, Paul quotes the book of Genesis to prove his point that Abraham was justified by faith:

"For what does the Scripture say? 'ABRAHAM BELIEVED GOD, AND IT WAS CREDITED TO HIM AS RIGHTEOUSNESS.' Now to the one who works, his wage is not credited as a favor, but as what is due. But to the one who does not work, but believes in Him who justifies the ungodly, his faith is credited as righteousness . . ."

Galatians
Solid Truth for Slippery Times

LOOKING EVEN CLOSER . . .
OBSERVE the TEXT of SCRIPTURE

READ Galatians 5:7-12 and **MARK** references to negative influences on the Galatians.

Galatians 5:7-12

7   You were running well; who hindered you from obeying the truth?

8   This persuasion did not come from Him who calls you.

9   A little leaven leavens the whole lump of dough.

10   I have confidence in you in the Lord that you will adopt no other view; but the one who is disturbing you will bear his judgment, whoever he is.

11   But I, brethren, if I still preach circumcision, why am I still persecuted? Then the stumbling block of the cross has been abolished.

12   I wish that those who are troubling you would even mutilate themselves.

DISCUSS with your GROUP or PONDER on your own . . .

How had the Galatians started off?

How did they go off course?

What do you need to know to obey the truth? (Make it simple.)

What hinders you from obeying the truth?

Can a church that doesn't *know* the truth *obey* the truth? What implications does this have for us?

What other forces were involved in the Galatians situation?

Did it take a lot of error to throw them off? What metaphor does Paul use to explain this?

ONE STEP FURTHER:

Word Study: *Peitho*
If you have extra time this week, find the three occurrences of the *peitho* word group in Galatians 5:7-12. Explore this word group in the New Testament then record your observations below.

Galatians
Solid Truth for Slippery Times

How does Paul further explain what "leaven" refers to in the context?

Have you seen "a little leaven work"? Explain.

How do we combat bad leaven?

How do you teach others to be careful of leaven without creating cynical/fearful thinkers?

Why is the cross called a stumbling block?

How does preaching circumcision and other works abolish the offense of the cross?

ONE STEP FURTHER:

Who is really calling you?
In verse 8 Paul says, "This persuasion *did* not *come* from Him who calls you." In Galatians 1:6 we were told about the true calling from God by the grace of Christ. Does persuasion to believe lies exist today? How do people deceive and why do they do it? How adept are you at distinguishing God's voice from the voice of imposters? How can you discern and stand firm?

How does Paul describe his opposition? What characterizes them? What does he wish they'd do to themselves?

Although Paul uses strong words, what indication do we have that he thinks he will be heard?

How do you approach situations where truth has been attacked?

What can we learn from Paul's situation?

Are there other things we need to consider before we speak?

ONE STEP FURTHER:

Jesus Talked about Leaven, Too

Jesus told His disciples to beware of the leaven of the Pharisees and the Sadducees. If you have some extra time this week, see what you can discover about leaven—both in the Old Testament and the New Testament. Record your findings below.

ONE STEP FURTHER:

The Cross

If you have some extra time this week, consider how the cross is described elsewhere in Scripture. In Galatians, Paul refers to it as "a stumbling block." How else is it talked about in the New Testament and what implications are there for us? Record your observations below.

Galatians
Solid Truth for Slippery Times

Digging Deeper

The Flesh and the Spirit in the New Testament

If you have some extra time this week, survey the New Testament to see what else is said about the difference between the flesh and the Spirit. Here are some critical passages to get you started, but don't feel limited by them as there are more out there!

Matthew 26:41, Mark 14:38

John 3

Romans 8

Ephesians 6

1 Peter 3–4

Summary:

LOOKING EVEN CLOSER . . .
OBSERVE the TEXT of SCRIPTURE

READ Galatians 5:13-26 and **MARK** references to the ways of *the Spirit* and *the flesh*.

Galatians 5:13-26

13 *For you were called to freedom, brethren; only do not turn your freedom into an opportunity for the flesh, but through love serve one another.*

14 *For the whole Law is fulfilled in one word, in the statement, "YOU SHALL LOVE YOUR NEIGHBOR AS YOURSELF."*

15 *But if you bite and devour one another, take care that you are not consumed by one another.*

16 *But I say, walk by the Spirit, and you will not carry out the desire of the flesh.*

17 *For the flesh sets its desire against the Spirit, and the Spirit against the flesh; for these are in opposition to one another, so that you may not do the things that you please.*

18 *But if you are led by the Spirit, you are not under the Law.*

19 *Now the deeds of the flesh are evident, which are: immorality, impurity, sensuality,*

20 *idolatry, sorcery, enmities, strife, jealousy, outbursts of anger, disputes, dissensions, factions,*

21 *envying, drunkenness, carousing, and things like these, of which I forewarn you, just as I have forewarned you, that those who practice such things will not inherit the kingdom of God.*

22 *But the fruit of the Spirit is love, joy, peace, patience, kindness, goodness, faithfulness,*

23 *gentleness, self-control; against such things there is no law.*

24 *Now those who belong to Christ Jesus have crucified the flesh with its passions and desires.*

25 *If we live by the Spirit, let us also walk by the Spirit.*

26 *Let us not become boastful, challenging one another, envying one another.*

DISCUSS with your GROUP or PONDER on your own . . .

What topic does Paul bring front and center again?

How does he address concerns about unrestrained freedom running amok?

What characterizes and drives the freedom of those in Christ?

What does Paul tell his readers to do in this section? (We're looking for statements made in the imperative mood.)

What does Paul contrast in this section? What two ways are there to live? How do they relate to one another?

Make a simple list comparing the deeds of the flesh with the fruit of the Spirit.

Deeds of the Flesh	Fruit of the Spirit

What results from walking by the Spirit?

You've already listed the deeds of the flesh. What commonalities do you see among them?

Do any of them group together? If so, how?

Galatians
Solid Truth for Slippery Times

What "deeds of the flesh" can you identify with?

What is the difference between doing a deed of the flesh and "practic[ing] such things"?

Is it evident when people are "practicing" such things?

By contrast, what characterizes a person who walks by the Spirit?

How do those who belong to Jesus deal with the flesh according to verse 24? What does this mean? (As you answer, be sure to consider Galatians 2:20.)

When Paul says, "If we live by the Spirit, let us also walk by the Spirit," what spiritual events is he referring to?

What does Paul say with regard to "one another" in verse 26? Does anything else in this section point to unrest between people within the Church?

How are Christians *not* to treat one another?

Do you ever have problems in this regard? Why do you think this is?

What practical steps can you take to combat this?

@THE END OF THE DAY . . .

After several chapters of hard-hitting truth, Paul dives into hard-hitting application. As you close your week of study, look back over the pages of Scripture you've been in this week and decide what your biggest application point in a chapter of application is. Ask God to cement one key truth to your heart and then record it below so you don't forget.

Galatians
Solid Truth for Slippery Times

Don't Grow Weary!

Let us not lose heart in doing good, for in due time we will reap if we do not grow weary.
–Galatians 6:9

Even when we live by the Spirit, we will still face trials and hardships in this life. We still live on a battleground with an enemy who seeks to steal, kill and destroy. While we live with the power of the indwelling Spirit, there are still burdens to bear and battles to fight. Over time weariness can set in.

In this closing chapter, Paul encourages his readers to keep on keeping on in the faith and gives a final warning about the troublemakers who have been compelling them to be circumcised so they can boast in their flesh.

Modern-day troublemakers don't compel circumcision, but their ilk still slinks around and you can still spot them by their "compelling" ways.

REMEMBERING

Take a few minutes to summarize Galatians 1–5. Include a theme for each chapter and a one- or two-sentence summary.

Galatians 1

Galatians 2

Galatians 3

Galatians 4

Galatians 5

WEEKLY READ-THROUGH #1

Version I read:

New observations/questions:

Version I read:

New observations/questions:

SETTING the SCENE

Having just concluded Galatians 5 by contrasting the deeds of the flesh with the fruit of the Spirit, Paul opens Galatians 6 with both still in view.

GALATIANS 6
OBSERVE the TEXT of SCRIPTURE

READ Galatians 6 and **MARK** key, repeated words in a distinctive fashion.

Galatians 6

1 *Brethren, even if anyone is caught in any trespass, you who are spiritual, restore such a one in a spirit of gentleness; each one looking to yourself, so that you too will not be tempted.*

2 *Bear one another's burdens, and thereby fulfill the law of Christ.*

3 *For if anyone thinks he is something when he is nothing, he deceives himself.*

4 *But each one must examine his own work, and then he will have reason for boasting in regard to himself alone, and not in regard to another.*

5 *For each one will bear his own load.*

Galatians
Solid Truth for Slippery Times

6   *The one who is taught the word is to share all good things with the one who teaches him.*

7   *Do not be deceived, God is not mocked; for whatever a man sows, this he will also reap.*

8   *For the one who sows to his own flesh will from the flesh reap corruption, but the one who sows to the Spirit will from the Spirit reap eternal life.*

9   *Let us not lose heart in doing good, for in due time we will reap if we do not grow weary.*

10 *So then, while we have opportunity, let us do good to all people, and especially to those who are of the household of the faith.*

11 *See with what large letters I am writing to you with my own hand.*

12 *Those who desire to make a good showing in the flesh try to compel you to be circumcised, simply so that they will not be persecuted for the cross of Christ.*

13 *For those who are circumcised do not even keep the Law themselves, but they desire to have you circumcised so that they may boast in your flesh.*

14 *But may it never be that I would boast, except in the cross of our Lord Jesus Christ, through which the world has been crucified to me, and I to the world.*

15 *For neither is circumcision anything, nor uncircumcision, but a new creation.*

16 *And those who will walk by this rule, peace and mercy be upon them, and upon the Israel of God.*

17 *From now on let no one cause trouble for me, for I bear on my body the brand-marks of Jesus.*

18 *The grace of our Lord Jesus Christ be with your spirit, brethren. Amen.*

DISCUSS with your GROUP or PONDER on your own . . .

How does Galatians 6 tie in with the preceding verses and chapters?

What key words did you notice?

Pick Your Key Verses

If you have time this week, pick a key verse from each chapter of Galatians to help you remember the content. Record your selections below.

Galatians 1

Galatians 2

Galatians 3

Galatians 4

Galatians 5

Galatians 6

What continuing contrasts does Paul use in this section?

What is the basic thought flow of Galatians 6?

What 5 W and H questions do you have for this section of the text?

LOOKING EVEN CLOSER . . .
OBSERVE the TEXT of SCRIPTURE

READ Galatians 6:1-10 and **MARK** *deceive* and *think/examine.*

Galatians 6:1-10

1   *Brethren, even if anyone is caught in any trespass, you who are spiritual, restore such a one in a spirit of gentleness; each one looking to yourself, so that you too will not be tempted.*

2   *Bear one another's burdens, and thereby fulfill the law of Christ.*

3   *For if anyone thinks he is something when he is nothing, he deceives himself.*

4   *But each one must examine his own work, and then he will have reason for boasting in regard to himself alone, and not in regard to another.*

5   *For each one will bear his own load.*

6   *The one who is taught the word is to share all good things with the one who teaches him.*

7   *Do not be deceived, God is not mocked; for whatever a man sows, this he will also reap.*

Galatians
Solid Truth for Slippery Times

8 *For the one who sows to his own flesh will from the flesh reap corruption,
but the one who sows to the Spirit will from the Spirit reap eternal life.*

9 *Let us not lose heart in doing good, for in due time we will reap if we do not
grow weary.*

10 *So then, while we have opportunity, let us do good to all people, and
especially to those who are of the household of the faith.*

DISCUSS with your GROUP or PONDER on your own . . .

What indication do we have that Paul thinks they will accept his words?

What situation does Paul address in the first verses of Galatians 6?

With what attitude should we approach a brother who sins?

Have you ever been in a situation that called for restoration? If so, what was your
attitude like? Was it easy? Hard? Explain.

In restoring another person, what safeguards do we need to consider?

Besides falling into the same sin, does the text mention other dangers?

What different pitfalls are described in this section?

What about instructions? What does Paul tell believers to do?

What does Paul warn his readers *not* to do?

What command in Galatians 5 is related to Paul's command in Galatians 6:2 to "Bear one another's burdens, and thereby fulfill the law of Christ"? Explain.

Have you ever lost heart in doing good or grown weary in sowing? Explain. How can we keep from growing weary and losing heart?

How can you encourage and help those you minister to and those who minister to you to keep from growing weary and losing heart?

What deceptions does Paul warn about?

Have you been deceived in either of these two ways? Explain.

What principle does Paul lay out in this section? How does this show that God cannot be mocked?

What people groups does Paul tell his readers to serve? How are they to serve?

What do we learn about time in this section?

How are you with regard to time? Do you seize opportunities to do good?

How can you improve in using your time for God's service and glory?

Do you trust God to cause you to reap in due time? Do you struggle with "due time" not being quite soon enough for you? Why? Just asking.

Galatians
Solid Truth for Slippery Times

Digging Deeper

Deception

Paul warns the Galatians not to deceive themselves into thinking they're something when they're nothing. He also warns them not to be deceived into thinking they can sow one thing and reap another. Knowing that our adversary is marked by deception, it's critical that we know what to watch for so that we will not be deceived. If you have some extra time this week, let's examine this further. Be sure to answer your questions from Scripture.

What do we know about our adversary, specifically with reference to his lying and deceiving?

How do Christians deceive themselves according to Scripture?

How does Satan seek to deceive people?

What other deceptions and lies do we need to be on guard against?

LOOKING EVEN CLOSER . . .
OBSERVE the TEXT of SCRIPTURE

READ Galatians 6:11-18 and **MARK** *boast* and *flesh*.

Galatians 6:11-18

11 See with what large letters I am writing to you with my own hand.

12 Those who desire to make a good showing in the flesh try to compel you to be circumcised, simply so that they will not be persecuted for the cross of Christ.

13 For those who are circumcised do not even keep the Law themselves, but they desire to have you circumcised so that they may boast in your flesh.

14 But may it never be that I would boast, except in the cross of our Lord Jesus Christ, through which the world has been crucified to me, and I to the world.

15 For neither is circumcision anything, nor uncircumcision, but a new creation.

16 And those who will walk by this rule, peace and mercy be upon them, and upon the Israel of God.

17 From now on let no one cause trouble for me, for I bear on my body the brand-marks of Jesus.

18 The grace of our Lord Jesus Christ be with your spirit, brethren. Amen.

Deceives

The word Paul uses for "deceives" (v. 3) is *phrenapatao*. It is a compound word that combines the word for "mind" (*phren*) and the word for "deceive" (*apatao*). Lies are an attack on the mind.

DISCUSS with your GROUP or PONDER on your own . . .

What personal notation marks a change in verse 11?

What topic does Paul revisit as he closes his letter?

Week Six: **Don't Grow Weary!**

What do the Judaizers want? What do they do? Why do they do it?

What similar behaviors should we beware of today?

Knowing yourself, do you think you are more prone to be compelled to wrong behavior or to compel someone else to it? How can you properly guard against your disposition?

What did preaching the cross do to Paul? What can we expect when we preach Christ crucified?

What does the cross do for the believer according to verse 14? What benefit does this bring in the here and now? Explain. Do you live in this reality?

What is the key issue according to Paul? Does circumcision or uncircumcision matter? Why?

Digging Deeper

The Cross

Why is the cross so important? Spend some time this week considering this question for yourself.

What do we learn in the Gospel accounts?

How does the Old Testament point ahead to it?

What is Paul's teaching?

What do other New Testament writers have to say?

How would you explain the centrality of the cross of Jesus Christ?

FYI:

Proper Boasting

For consider your calling, brethren, that there were not many wise according to the flesh, not many mighty, not many noble; but God has chosen the foolish things of the world to shame the wise, and God has chosen the weak things of the world to shame the things which are strong, and the base things of the world and the despised God has chosen, the things that are not, so that He may nullify the things that are, so that no man may boast before God. But by His doing you are in Christ Jesus, who became to us wisdom from God, and righteousness and sanctification, and redemption, so that, just as it is written, "Let him who boasts, boast in the Lord."

—1 Corinthians 1:26-31

Who is Paul referring to in the phrase "the Israel of God"? Explain your answer.

What brand-marks of Jesus did Paul bear on his body? What does this say about him?

What brand-marks of Jesus do you bear?

@THE END OF THE DAY . . .

As you finish your time of study this week, take some time to think back over the whole Galatians letter. What is your biggest takeaway from this study? What truth or truths will most change the way you think and act moving forward? Give yourself adequate time to think and pray through this and then jot down below the key points you want to remember.

RESOURCES

Helpful Study Tools

The New How to Study Your Bible
Eugene, Oregon: Harvest House
Publishers

The New Inductive Study Bible
Eugene, Oregon: Harvest House
Publishers

Logos Bible Software
Available at www.logos.com.

Greek Word Study Tools

Kittel, G., Friedrich, G., & Bromiley,
G.W.
*Theological Dictionary of the New
Testament, Abridged* (also known as
Little Kittel)
Grand Rapids, Michigan: W.B.
Eerdmans Publishing Company

Zodhiates, Spiros
*The Complete Word Study Dictionary:
New Testament*
Chattanooga, Tennessee: AMG
Publishers

Hebrew Word Study Tools

Harris, R.L., Archer, G.L., & Walker,
B.K.
*Theological Wordbook of the Old
Testament* (also known as TWOT)
Chicago, Illinois: Moody Press

Zodhiates, Spiros
*The Complete Word Study Dictionary:
Old Testament*
Chattanooga, Tennessee: AMG
Publishers

General Word Study Tools

Strong, James
*The New Strong's Exhaustive
Concordance of the Bible*
Nashville, Tennessee: Thomas Nelson

Recommended Commentary Sets

Expositor's Bible Commentary
Grand Rapids, Michigan: Zondervan

NIV Application Commentary
Grand Rapids, Michigan: Zondervan

The New American Commentary
Nashville, Tennessee: Broadman and
Holman Publishers

One-Volume Commentary

Carson, D.A., France, R.T., Motyer,
J.A., & Wenham, G.J. Ed.
*New Bible Commentary: 21st Century
Edition*
Downers Grove, Illinois: Inter-Varsity
Press

Exegetical Commentary on Galatians

Bruce, F.F.
*The Epistle to the Galatians:
A Commentary on the Greek Text*.
From the *New International Greek
Testament Commentary Series*
Grand Rapids, MI: W.B. Eerdmans
Publishing Company

For use with www.blueletterbible.org

1. Type in BIble verse. Change the version to NASB. Click the "Search" button.
2. When you arrive at the next screen, you will see six lettered boxes to the left of your verse. Click the "C" button to take you to the concordance link.
3. Click on the Strong's number which is the link to the original word in Greek or Hebrew.

Clicking this number will bring up another screen that will give you a brief definition of the word as well as list every occurrence of the Greek word in the New Testament or Hebrew word in the Old Testament. Before running to the dictionary definition, scan places where this word is used in Scripture and examine the general contexts where it is used.

ABOUT PRECEPT

Precept Ministries International was raised up by God for the sole purpose of establishing people in God's Word to produce reverence for Him. It serves as an arm of the church without respect to denomination. God has enabled Precept to reach across denominational lines without compromising the truths of His inerrant Word. We believe every word of the Bible was inspired and given to man as all that is necessary for him to become mature and thoroughly equipped for every good work of life. This ministry does not seek to impose its doctrines on others, but rather to direct people to the Master Himself, who leads and guides by His Spirit into all truth through a systematic study of His Word. The ministry produces a variety of Bible studies and holds conferences and intensive Training Workshops designed to establish attendees in the Word through Inductive Bible Study.

Jack Arthur and his wife, Kay, founded Precept Ministries in 1970. Kay and the ministry staff of writers produce **Precept Upon Precept** studies, **In & Out** studies, **Lord** series studies, the **New Inductive Study Series** studies, **40-Minute** studies, and **Discover 4 Yourself Inductive Bible Studies for Kids**. From years of diligent study and teaching experience, Kay and the staff have developed these unique, inductive courses that are now used in nearly 185 countries and 70 languages.

 PRECEPT.ORG

GET CONNECTED

LEARN HOW you can get involved in "Establishing People in God's Word" at precept.org/connect

 Use your smartphone to connect to Precept's ministry initiatives. **Precept.org/connect**

PRECEPT ONLINE COMMUNITY provides support, training opportunities and exclusive resources to help Bible study leaders and students. Connect at Precept Online Community at Precept.org/POC.

 Use your smartphone to connect to Precept Online Community. **Precept.org/POC**

Galatians
Solid Truth for Slippery Times

PAM GILLASPIE

Pam Gillaspie, a passionate Bible student and teacher, authors Precept's *Sweeter Than Chocolate!*® and *Cookies on the Lower Shelf*™ Bible study series. Pam holds a BA in Biblical Studies from Wheaton College in Wheaton, Illinois. She and her husband live in suburban Chicago, Illinois with their son, daughter, and Great Dane. Her greatest joy is encouraging others to read God's Word widely and study it deeply . . . precept upon precept.

Connect with Pam at:

www.deepandwide.org

 pamgillaspie

 pamgillaspie

CPSIA information can be obtained
at www.ICGtesting.com
Printed in the USA
BVHW07s2058220818
525302BV00015B/540/P